To

Robert Hormats

with best regards,

Sumen Kandhari

2/17/89

INTERNATIONAL CAPITAL MARKETS

NEW DIRECTIONS

Edited by
Surendra K. Kaushik, PhD
Lubin Graduate School of Business
Pace University

New York Institute of Finance

Library of Congress Cataloging-in-Publication Data

International capital markets.

Bibliography: p.
Includes index.
1. Capital market. 2. International finance.
3. Banks and banking, International. I. Kaushik,
S. K., 1944-
HG4523.I58 1988 332'.042 88-25387
ISBN 0-13-472481-X

This publication is designed to provide accurate and authoritative information in regard to the subject matter covered. It is sold with the understanding that the publisher is not engaged in rendering legal, accounting, or other professional service. If legal advice or other expert assistance is required, the services of a competent professional person should be sought.

From a Declaration of Principles Jointly Adopted by a Committee of the American Bar Association and a Committee of Publishers and Associations

A Division of Simon & Schuster, Inc
70 Pine Street, New York, NY 10270-0003

Printed in the United States of America

10 9 8 7 6 5 4 3 2 1

New York Institute of Finance
(NYIF Corp.)
70 Pine Street
New York, New York 10270-0003

Dedicated to the memory of
my father, Laxminarain Kaushik

CONTENTS

FOREWORD

ISSUES IN INTERNATIONAL BANKING AND FINANCE

Leonard Silk

Dr. Leonard Silk is the Economics Columnist of The New York Times *and Distinguished Professor of Economics at Pace University's Lubin Graduate School of Business. He received his AB degree at the University of Wisconsin in 1940 and his PhD at Duke University in 1947. He has taught at Duke, the University of Maine, Simmons College, New York University, and Columbia University. Dr. Silk has written several books and received various honors, including the Loeb Award for Distinguished Business and Financial Journalism in 1961, 1966, 1967, 1971, and 1978. He is also a member of the Council on Foreign Relations.*

Issues in International Banking and Finance

The stock market crash of October 1987, which began in Wall Street and spread almost instantaneously throughout the world, dramatized the new and dangerously unstable world in which we live. It heightened awareness of the linkages between international banking and financial markets on one side and prospects for the world economy on the other. Among the participants at the March 1988 Pace University conference on international banking, it intensified interest in the agenda for reform involving exchange rates, interest rates, fiscal and monetary policies, trade policy and protectionism, capital flows among nations, and of the huge and still growing volume of world debt, including not only that of the less developed countries but of the United States, now the world's biggest debtor by far.

Although the immediate anxiety created by the October stock market crash has begun to fade, we will have only ourselves to blame if we treat it merely as an accident, a massive quirk, a big noise signifying nothing or very little, rather than as a warning of the need to strengthen the world financial system.

The threat to the system has been a long time in the making: "The postwar growth of the world economy has depended overwhelmingly on the strength of the U.S. economy and the dollar."[1] Paradoxically, it has also depended on American balance of payments deficits, which were the source of growing monetary reserves essential to expanding world trade. Behind the threat to the international system lay a contradiction first pointed out three decades ago by Robert Triffin: A strong dollar and chronic U.S. payments deficits could not indefinitely coexist; either the dollar would weaken and the system would break down, or the American payments deficit would end, the supply of monetary reserves would contract, and economic expansion of the system would cease.

The Bretton Woods fixed-exchange rate system, established at the end of World War II, did break down in 1972-1973. With the switch to floating exchange rates, however, the world economy managed to weather the oil shocks and inflation of the 1970s. The United States continued to run current-account payments deficits, which worsened during the Reagan years, driven by the rapidly widening budget deficits. Nevertheless, the dollar remained the world's principal currency and the United States the chief provider of military protection for the noncommunist world. The monetary system survived, if in a somewhat precarious state, with the American payments deficits covered by capital inflow from abroad. Foreign governments were eager to prevent both a collapse of the dollar and a withdrawal of the United States from its defense commitments. Nor did the United States itself want to give up the key-currency role for the dollar or its political-military hegemony, despite the heavy costs.

One of the costs has been a highly volatile dollar and world currency system. The Reagan administration has played Hamlet on the dollar, wavering between measures to support it or to let it fall. When concerns about the trade deficit--and the fear that Congress will swing to a protectionist policy--rise, the administration lets the dollar slide. When worries about the securities markets or a drop in foreign capital inflow increase, the U.S. government moves to stabilize the dollar. Many analysts continue to fear that, in the longer run, the dollar will fall and inflict grave damage on the American and world economy.

There is no sure bottom for the dollar if U.S. fiscal and monetary policies are overly stimulative. That would cause imports to stay high and would prevent an adequate expansion of exports. Fear of a falling dollar would undermine foreign private investors' confidence, and they would stay away from dollar investments. If foreign respect for U.S. fiscal responsibility deteriorates further (it has not been high for the last few years), foreign central banks might be unwilling to continue to support the dollar. The result would be a spectacular exchange crisis and a sell-off of dollar assets. United States interest rates would be driven sky-high, the stock and bond markets would be driven down, and the economy would fall into severe recession or depression.

Economic forecasting is--like all the sciences, but more than most --probabilistic, and one cannot be certain that a crash landing would be the inevitable outcome of fiscal carelessness. But so great are the risks that, in my view, it would be far wiser to adopt a strategy that would curb further the decline of the dollar. This would require a tougher budget policy and a firm monetary policy; the tougher the fiscal restraints, the easier monetary policy could be, without exciting worries about renewed inflation. The resulting decline in interest rates would help keep the economy moving forward.

The critical difference between the two possible approaches--benign neglect of the dollar based on belief in a self-stabilizing dollar versus the defense of the dollar to prevent a major crisis of confidence--lies in the assumptions made about the links between the foreign exchange market and the financial markets.

In the benign-neglect view, the dollar's fall will be self-limiting, as it restores equilibrium in the U.S. current-account balance of payments, and will therefore have no deleterious effects on interest rates and securities prices. In the other view, a falling dollar, unless arrested by policy actions, will eventually trigger a collapse in the U.S. credit and securities markets. The rising rates of interest will not only hurt the American economy but make it increasingly difficult for foreign countries to service their debts, with extremely harmful consequences for American and other Western banks. Some key money-center and regional banks are already in plenty of trouble because of their heavy exposure to questionable foreign debt.

Which view of the falling dollar is the more likely to be correct? The experience of the past two years throws light on the question. In early 1986, the dollar unexpectedly lost 11% of its value against the German mark in only six weeks. Although the dollar had been declining irregularly for nearly a year, there had not previously been so steep a drop or so adverse a reaction in the U.S. bond market. This time, however, the bond market plunged. In late April 1986, it lost more than 7 points. At the time, it was the largest one-week fall in memory.

Until 1986, foreign investors had been willing to buy U.S. bonds and other dollar assets despite the falling dollar. Why? Because the advantage in the interest-rate differential or the expected capital gains on dollar investments over those in other currencies was considered sufficient to offset the exchange risk. Then, in January 1986, as the dollar fell, foreign investors' assessment of the exchange risk worsened, with two effects. One was that many investors, unwilling to buy more dollar securities or even hold all those they already owned without hedging the exchange risk, suddenly did hedge by borrowing dollars from banks in the United States or abroad. They then sold the borrowed dollars for hard foreign currencies such as the yen, the German mark, or the Swiss franc. The surge of demand for dollar credit drove up short-term interest rates in the United States and the Eurodollar market and thrust the dollar down.

The second effect was on the U.S. bond market. The suddenly perceived exchange risk knocked bond prices down and raised U.S. long-term interest rates. Fear of rising import prices to the United States and of inflation stemming from the falling dollar further lifted long-term interest rates. The process by which weakening confidence in the dollar lifts American interest rates and depresses asset prices, which is so well understood and feared in financial markets, appears to be ignored or minimized elsewhere, including by academic economists. This process works automatically. It does not depend on any action by the Federal Reserve to tighten credit. The Federal Reserve can, of course, resist the rise of short-term interest rates if it so chooses by injecting reserves into American banks, but the effect on long-term rates may be perverse, because the effect of a large injection of liquidity breeds fear of inflation and raises long-term rates and drives down bond prices. The feedback effect is then likely to be a further undermining of confidence in the dollar and exacerbated inflationary expectations.

The dollar's plunge in January to March 1986 was precipitated by the Federal Reserve, whose monetary policy had been expansive all through 1985; nevertheless, business investment and housing had faltered. Investment was squeezed between high real interest rates as a result of the massive federal budget deficit and falling profits in agriculture and manufacturing, aggravated by the flood of low-priced imports and the loss of export markets. The Federal Reserve was under heavy pressure from the administration and from manufacturing, housing, and farm interests to try to remedy the situation by opening the money tap wider. Indeed, the money supply took off, with M1 accelerating from 11.5% in 1985 to nearly 17% in 1986.[2]

In this expansive monetary environment, the dollar was bound to go on falling. Early in the autumn of 1986, signs of trouble reappeared as confidence in the dollar waned and foreigners again began to borrow dollars heavily to hedge commercial and investment positions. Short-term rates turned up and were soon followed by long-term rates. By the spring of 1987, a full-fledged crisis was in progress. Treasury bond prices plummeted, and net private foreign purchases of dollars fell to zero and below, as purchases of U.S. securities were offset by short-term bank outflows reflecting borrowing to hedge dollar exposures.

To finance the trade deficit and slow the dollar's fall, foreign central banks had to step into the breach and absorb dollars in the amount of an estimated $70 billion in the five months, January to May 1987. Thereafter, the financing of the U.S. trade deficit was in the hands of the central banks, particularly of the Bank of Japan.

In May 1987, this second round of the ongoing dollar crisis abated, as the U.S. trade deficit showed signs of improving. The Federal Reserve had helped out by tightening a bit to reassure the markets, but the results did not last long. Within a couple of months, the U.S. trade balance worsened again, as domestic demand picked up in a lagged response to monetary ease in 1986. Imports climbed, and soon the dollar was under renewed pressure. Interest rates again took off, soaring to another peak in mid-October 1987. And this time the stock market got into the act, unlike the two preceding credit-market crunches.

In the spring 1986 and spring 1987 crunches, Wall Street had undergone what stockbrokers like to call a "correction," but so great was the market's momentum that it soon recovered and climbed to new highs. This time the market peaked out in August 1987, and the crash of October 19 followed. Close market observers have not the slightest doubts that the needle that pricked the bubble was the news report of an unexpectedly bad trade report and Treasury Secretary James Baker's remarks implying that the central banks' February 1987 agreement (the Louvre Accord) to stabilize the dollar was no longer binding. The tight link between the exchange and financial markets was thus confirmed.

Given that link--and the underlying links between the nation's fiscal deficit, trade deficit, dependence on foreign capital inflows, and the upward pressure on prices and interest rates--an overhaul of U.S. economic policies is crucial to avoid a further weakening of the dollar and a blow to the international monetary system and our banking institutions. This book explores the complex interrelationships of these factors and offers thoughtful proposals for remedying the ills of the existing system and thereby warding off the clear and present dangers to our banks and our entire economy at home and abroad. As recent events have proved, a sharp distinction between the domestic and international economy and financial markets can no longer be made.

Notes

[1] I wish to express my deepest thanks to David M. Calleo of the Johns Hopkins University and Harold van Buren Cleveland, formerly of Citicorp, for their help. See D. Calleo, H. Cleveland, and L. Silk, "The Dollar and the Defense of the West," *Foreign Affairs*, Spring 1988.

[2] M1 consists of: (1) currency outside the U.S. Treasury, Federal Reserve Banks, and the vaults of depository institutions; (2) travelers checks of nonbank issuers; (3) demand deposits at all commercial banks other than those due to depository institutions, the U.S. government, and foreign banks and official institutions, less cash items in the process of collection and Federal Reserve float; and (4) other checkable deposits (OCDs), consisting of negotiable order of withdrawal (NOW) and automatic transfer service (ATS) accounts at depository institutions, credit union share draft accounts, and demand deposits at thrift institutions. Seasonally adjusted M1 is calculated by summing currency, travelers checks, demand deposits, and OCDs, each seasonally adjusted separately.

ACKNOWLEDGMENTS

Pace University and its Lubin Graduate School of Business were most supportive of the conference for which these papers were written: Dr. Edward J. Mortola, chancellor; Dr. William G. Sharwell, president and chief executive officer; Dr. Joseph M. Pastore, Jr., provost; and Dr. George M. "Chip" Parks, dean, Lubin Schools of Business (the Graduate School and the School of Business Administration), were personally generous with their time and encouragement. Dr. John T. McCall, vice provost for administration, and Dr. Arthur Centonze, associate dean, Lubin Graduate School of Business, were very helpful in preparations for the conference.

CBS, Inc. and Chicago Mercantile Exchange (CME) provided generous financial support through the offices of Mr. Fred J. Meyer and Mr. Lawrence M. Krackov at CBS, and Dr. Ira G. Kawaller at CME.

The conference could not have been possible without the participation of Mr. Sam Y. Cross, Dr. Stephen C. Eyre, Dr. Irving S. Friedman, Dr. Jeffrey E. Garten, Mr. Robert M. Giordano, Dr. Ira G. Kawaller, Dr. Ronald I. McKinnon, Mme. Helene Ploix, Dr. Jeffrey M. Schaefer, Mr. Philip D. Sherman, Dr. Leonard Silk, Dr. David G. Strongin, Mr. Andre A.L. Swings, Dr. Robert Triffin, and Mr. John Winthrop Wright.

Much is owed to business executives, professors, students, and public officials whose participation made the undertaking of the symposium worthwhile.

Dr. Fred N. Silverman, professor of management science, gave most generously of his time and talent in computer usage from the beginning of the project to the publication of this book. Dr. Verne S. Atwater, director, Center for the Study of Financial Services, Dr. Clarke C. Johnson, chairman, Dr. Raymond Lopez, and Dr. Barnard Seligman, all professors in the finance department of the Lubin Graduate School of Business, were most supportive of the activities of the Institute of International Banking. Dr. William C. Freund, the New York Stock Exchange Professor and Chairman, Department of Economics, Lubin Graduate School of Business, Pace University, was a valuable resource. Dr. Robert Vambery, professor of international business, and director, Center for International Business Studies, was also helpful. Dr. Warren Keegan, professor of international business, and director, Institute for Global Business Strategy, is always interested, supportive, and enthusiastic about the Institute's programs and publications. Professor F. Taylor Ostrander always brings his rich experience in government and international business to the deliberations of the Institute.

Many individuals in the university provided support services: Ms. Ellyn Doris, Ms. Jane Lawentman, Ms. Marie Ryder, Ms. Dawn Knipe, Mr. Bela Danville, Ms. Gina Logomarsino, Ms. Jackie Myers, Ms. Lisa Perriello, Ms. Ana Rivera, and Ms. Edna Laino.

Five research assistants worked on the conference and the book: Mr. Aniruddha Chakraborty ("Benson"), Mr. David Kogan, Mr.

Stephen Jones, and Mr. Rajendra Dhanasar provided assistance during the conference. Ms. Tracy Angerame provided superb help in using Ventura Publisher and in preparing the bibliography. Her assistance was critical in finishing the book on time.

Ms. Alberta Buchanan is one person who has been part of this book from conception of the conference idea to the word processing with Microsoft Word and preparation of manuscript for publication of the book. None of this would have happened without her painstaking effort over a period of 10 months.

Mr. Fred Dahl, director, publishing, Mr. Fred Eickelberg, director, marketing, Ms. Jeanmarie Brusati, manager, production, and Ms. Barbara Marino, copy editor, at the New York Institute of Finance deserve much credit for the timely publication of the ideas in these pages.

INTRODUCTION

Surendra K. Kaushik

Dr. Kaushik is professor of finance and director of the Institute of International Banking at the Lubin Graduate School of Business, Pace University. Before joining Pace, he taught at Babson College, Northeastern University, Boston State College, Lowell University, and Boston University. Dr. Kaushik's main areas of professional work are domestic and international financial markets. As director of the Institute of International Banking, he has started a series of publications, major conferences on international banking and finance, an active and close relationship with the banking industry, luncheon seminars, and corporate programs. He received his PhD in monetary economics from Boston University after earlier study at the University of Rajasthan, Jaipur, India.

International capital markets continue to play larger and larger roles in integrating the world economy. As a first effect, efficient allocation of financial resources is one major and obvious benefit that globalization of financial markets creates for savers and investors across national economies. The ultimate effect of increasing financial integration, therefore, on real resource allocation, product mix, comparative advantage, and trading patterns is significant. These import outcomes make stability and smooth functioning of financial markets on a global scale essential in today's high-tech environment when any change or disturbance in one market is instantly transmitted through all international capital markets. That is, any systemic risk emanating from participating agents in the markets needs to be managed while markets are allowed to integrate with one another.

Here the focus is on the first effect. An assessment of the overall international monetary and financial system and some of its key elements is offered by eminent experts and practitioners. The papers included were presented at the Fourth Conference on International Banking and Finance organized by the Institute of International Banking of the Lubin Graduate School of Business, Pace University, in New York City on March 31, 1988.

Adequacy of liquidity and available credit, and the functioning of the international monetary system is an important area of ongoing research, debate, and proposals for reform of the institutional structure. The papers in Part I address these issues. Growth of foreign exchange markets, behavior of foreign exchange rates, and some of the ways to minimize risks associated with volatility in foreign exchange markets at the macro (policy) as well as micro (business) levels are the subjects of the papers in Part II. In Part III, papers dealing with international financial intermediation, capital flows, especially to the United States, and regulatory concerns regarding banking and securities markets in a globally integrated market environment are presented.

The issues, recent developments, and new directions covered in this volume deserve and continue to receive attention at the highest policy levels. The Toronto Economic Summit of June 19-21, 1988, for example, states in its declaration: "In the 1980s inflation has been brought under control, laying the basis for sustained strong growth and improved productivity. The result has been the longest period of economic growth in postwar history. However, the 1980s have seen the emergence of large external imbalances in the major industrial economies, greater exchange rate volatility, and debt servicing difficulties in a number of developing countries." It further states: "Our response to these developments has been an increased commitment to international cooperation, resulting in an intensified process of policy coordination adopted at the 1986 Tokyo summit and further strengthened at the Venice summit and in the Group of Seven." The summit's response to the problems it recognizes is international cooperation, which may or may not be sufficient. Some of the reforms suggested by the experts here may have to be implemented, while others are being adopted at different levels. For example, a monetary integration of Western Europe.

International Liquidity

Creation and managed expansion/contraction of international liquidity, in many of its facets, remains a problem area for the international monetary system (after its abandonment in 1971) as it was before the creation of the Bretton Woods system in 1945. Insufficient liquidity, currency convertibility, and disequilibrating capital movements in a system that revolves around the U. S. dollar continue to produce inflationary expectations and unstable exchange rates according to Irving Friedman. United States fiscal policy and inadequate savings, among others, are identified as factors contributing to instability. His analysis, based on long and wide-ranging experience with these questions, leads him to recommend a new framework for growth that will produce stable exchange rates, currency convertibility, and sufficient liquidity as against current conditions of currency devaluations and chronic external debt problems of developing countries. Although he has a gloomy business forecast for 1989-1991,

Friedman thinks the industrial countries and multilateral agencies, such as the International Monetary Fund (IMF) and the World Bank, together should be able to prevent liquidity crises. Some of the recommendations Friedman makes seem to be heeded again by commercial banks as evidenced by, for example, the new rescheduling agreement with Brazil as well as by the Paris Club, which has endorsed long maturities for existing debt and additional funding for the debt-ridden poor sub-Saharan African countries.

Robert Triffin approaches the liquidity problem from a somewhat different perspective, namely, that the U.S. dollar, a national currency, is used as an international currency. This "extravagant privilege" bestowed on the U.S. dollar by other countries is the root problem in the present international monetary system. At a practical level, Triffin illustrates the point through an examination of the international balance sheet of the United States. In particular, he points out huge capital imports by the United States. Triffin recommends that other countries should agree on institutional reform, pending U.S. participation.

Regional monetary agreements such as the European Monetary System and its European Currency Unit (ECU), which is already used by European governments for settlement of payments, should be used as parallel currency. The recent monetary agreement among European finance ministers to create a European unit of account along the lines of a reference currency rather than as a basket currency (current ECU) is a major step in putting in place Triffin's ideas of European monetary unification. The next step, that of creating a European central bank, is under serious consideration by the European Community, as West Germany is withdrawing its hitherto opposition to it. At the Hanover, West Germany summit of June 28, 1988, the European Community's heads of state agreed to set up a committee of central bankers and experts to study questions related to monetary union, including a European central bank, and to report its recommendations for concrete steps by 1989. These recent but very significant developments will ease the burden on the U.S. dollar as an international currency of denomination and thus not only supplement the payments system of the world but also reduce exchange rate volatility as world trade and capital movements are denominated in several parallel currencies.

Many experts and practitioners have been advocating elimination of exchange rate problems by creating a new international currency. The special Drawing Rights of the IMF have not achieved enough usage as a currency of denomination and payments settlement. Reformists like Richard N. Cooper of Harvard and John Winthrop Wright recommend a true international currency. Wright suggests, in this volume, an international currency unit (ICU) for this purpose. The international economic anarchy of the free-enterprise system should be brought under control through creation of an international bank to control liquidity and soundness of international finance, according to Wright.

Conclusions similar to Triffin's and Wright's are also arrived at by Andre A.L. Swings in that the volatile exchange rate of the dollar is due to limitations of a national currency in its role as an international currency. European integration, one European currency, and possibly a European central bank, will solve much of the liquidity and exchange rate problems experienced by the world economy in recent years. The U.S. dollar, Japanese yen, and a European currency would represent the three main parts of the world economy commensurate with their role in global industry, trade, and financial transactions.

Volatility in foreign exchange markets and the debt problems of developing countries have led many experts to call for international coordination of economic policies among the major industrial countries. The Group of Seven have responded positively to this idea and have put it into practice in recent years. The Group of Seven have again reaffirmed their resolve on cooperation and coordination during the recent Toronto summit. Another and a wider forum where coordination has received much attention is the International Monetary Fund. Helene Ploix presents IMF perspective on coordination and debt financing. There is much progress on both these issues according to Ploix. Coordination has resulted in the major countries assessing international consequences of domestic policies since the Bonn economic summit of 1978, but much more so since the Plaza Accord of September 1985. Similarly, debt financing and structural adjustment of developing countries are more systematic so that the poorest and the middle-income debtors are treated differently. Innovation in financing and adjustment methods at the Paris Club and by private capital markets including banks has been the hallmark of progress. The recent announcement (June 1988) by France to forgive debts of poorest African countries and reduced interest payments and lengthened repayment maturities for others have been followed by the G-7 agreeing to provide a better repayment schedule as well as more help to the poorest debtors. Even the United States has announced this recently when Treasury Secretary James Baker, III stated his concurrence with the G-7 on this issue. The middle-income countries, however, will continue to be treated on a case-by-case basis.

Foreign Exchange Markets

Innovations in foreign exchange markets, accounting for velocity in foreign exchange rates, the role of the federal budget deficit in exchange markets, and management of velocity through the use of futures and options instruments receive a closer look in this section. Growth in foreign exchange markets where trading volume is estimated to exceed $400 billion a day with a tremendous diversity in instruments and 24-hour trading have truly become global by 1988. The reality of global integration between financial markets is presented by Sam Cross. He also reminds the market participant, the policy maker, and the reader that the perspective of a connection between the production and exchange of goods and services on one hand, and all the financial transactions on the other, must be central to the international financial system. He also hints at some limit to systemic risks posed by financial integration. And he reports continuous surveillance and coordination on the part of central bankers. In conclusion, he echoes the optimism of Irving Friedman and Helene Ploix in the previous section.

A theoretical perspective on recent volatility in dollar exchange rate vis-a-vis the deutsche mark and the Japanese yen is provided by Ronald McKinnon. He concludes that tight money was not the cause of high U.S. interest rates in 1987 and recommends using interest-rate interpretation of a falling dollar. The U.S. policy should announce and support a floor for the dollar, according to McKinnon. The United States, Japan, and Germany should together act as anchor for the international monetary system by maintaining a competitive interest-rate policy to avoid exchange rate volatility.

The role of the U.S. budget deficit in exchange rate behavior through foreign financing is analyzed by Robert Giordano. He agrees with these economists, who take a macroeconomic perspective on capital imports to finance the deficit. In this perspective, the budget deficit remains a problem. The stock market crash of October 1987 probably was rooted in the budget deficit via the unwinding of capital inflows. "As long as this process continues, the financial markets remain exposed to a replay of the October events, even though any replay would likely be much less dramatic," according to Giordano.

A micro perspective on how to deal with the foreign exchange volatility is provided by Ira Kawaller in his paper. He gives examples of the use of futures and options instruments in foreign exchange. The Chicago Mercantile Exchange, where Kawaller develops new futures and options instruments, of course, is among the exchanges leading in futures and options instruments. Growth in the use of these instruments for hedging as well as speculating in currency markets has coincided with growth in volatility of exchange rates.

Banking and Securities Markets

A general and brief but poignant comment on foreign capital flows to the United States as a stable and attractive place to invest is made by Stephen Eyre. Turning to the international financial integration from the U.S. viewpoint, the Glass-Steagall separation of commercial and investment banking has become a nonissue according to Philip Sherman. He pays tribute to a combination of factors that have maintained healthy financial markets in Japan. Looking to the future, Sherman sees greater importance of functionality over institutional arrangement of financial players along with diversification of sources of funds on a global scale. International financial integration and competition are here, and the players have to provide financial services against that background.

A related point that resurfaces continuously is that concerning foreign capital inflows. Without reviewing the pros and cons, or the domestic and global consequences as analyzed in other papers, Jeffrey Schaefer and David G. Strongin present a most detailed account of foreign portfolio investment in the United States. This is precious information not widely available. Increase in total volume during the 1980s, shifts between equities and government securities, between short-term and long-term securities, and investor preferences, e.g., Japanese, European, British, etc., are highlighted to give a reality base to what is commonly called "globalization of financial markets."

The last article, by Jeffrey Garten, looks ahead into an area that few among policy makers, securities exchanges, and market participants have done. Garten cautions us against a limited view of the stock market crash of October 1987 and market and policy responses to it mainly from a domestic capital market approach. Integration of equity markets on a global scale is not yet here, but markets are moving in that direction. However, there is presently no institutional mechanism to deal with a potential securities market crisis on a global scale similar to coordination among central banks on banking and payments crises. He, therefore, sees an urgent need for a minimal regulation necessary for a smooth functioning of securities markets globally. To this end, Garten proposes a regulatory framework in which the Bank for International Settlements (BIS) may play a central role. Subsequent to presentation of his new and original ideas on March 31, 1988, Garten has also published its key parts in an article titled "We Need Global Regulations for Stocks" in *The New York Times* of June 12, 1988.

Together the papers in this volume give a coherent picture of international capital markets in many of their aspects and new directions. There is much in these papers that is of interest to policy makers, market participants, and students of the international financial system.

PART I

INTERNATIONAL LIQUIDITY

CHAPTER 1

THE WORLD ECONOMY AND THE INTERNATIONAL FINANCIAL SYSTEM

Irving S. Friedman

A graduate of Columbia University, Dr. Friedman has taught at All Souls College of Oxford, Yale, Virginia, and Fordham Universities. He has served at senior levels in the U.S. Treasury Department, the International Monetary Fund, the World Bank, the African, Asian, and Inter-American Banks, Citibank, First Boston Corporation, the Security Pacific Bank, the Society for International Development, and others in numerous capacities. He has written extensively on inflation, economic development, country assessment, the role of private banks in the developing world, the world debt problem, and other aspects of international economics and finance.

This paper outlines my views on the outlook for the world economy, giving first a brief summary of the global economy. This is followed by some thoughts on the outlook for the international monetary system.

A Gloomy Business Forecast for 1989-1991

We are headed for a serious recession in 1989 or 1990, irrespective of which party or candidate wins the presidential election in November 1988. Domestic demand will be weak, and unemployment will rise markedly. As for the balance of payments, relatively speaking, the United States will do well in improving its export performance. Imports will remain responsive to income and output conditions. This responsiveness will be fairly strong in 1988 but will decline in 1989-1990. Thus, the devaluation of the U.S. dollar will continue to have more visible effects on exports than on imports. Overseas demand will be weak at the same time, becoming seriously so as recession in the United States combines with an already slow growth in much of the Western world. Europe and Japan will have the international liquidity to finance a strong import demand, but their weak domestic demand will constrain their imports. In sharp contrast, the developing countries will have strong domestic demand, but their international liquidity shortages will curtail their demand for imports. This will be significant for the United States because of the major importance of developing countries as export markets for the United States. Thus, I see a serious world recession in 1989 or 1990, including the Pacific Rim countries as their foreign markets become more limited. On the financial side, the developing countries in the Pacific areas will be able to finance their imports and maintain debt servicing unless conditions in the developed countries result in further cutbacks in commercial lending to the presently creditworthy developing countries. Adverse global conditions could transform presently strong, creditworthy borrowers into weak debtors with dubious creditworthiness.

We dare not forget that in the late 1970s and into the 1980s (until the recession of 1981-1983), Brazil and Mexico were regarded by multilateral and private institutions as strong borrowers that were able to maintain their creditworthiness with private lenders. If world recession becomes deep and prolonged, the outcome for developing countries will be greatly influenced by whether the international community is prepared to respond quickly and adequately to defend growth and development in order to offset the inevitable increased cautiousness of private lenders. The international community will probably be prepared with more means to make this response than it had in 1981-1983. The multilateral agencies are being strengthened. The capital of the World Bank is likely to be increased as well as that of the African Development Bank and other regional banks. The International Monetary Fund (IMF) will probably obtain large increases although probably not enough. For many years (even when the fund had only about $50 billion), I have strongly advocated an IMF of at least $300 billion. We may see rather soon an IMF of $200 billion. Given the available liquidity of the major industrial nations, a fund of $200 billion should be able to prevent liquidity crises in developing countries that may result from the next recession. If the fund is not expanded in time, bilateral sources of official assistance may take front stage in importance. Japan and Germany seem to be well poised for such greatly expanded bilateral actions.

It may be argued that the industrial world knows how to avoid deep and prolonged recessions. I believe that it does. Nevertheless, I also believe that we will have a serious recession. We are paying the price of the continuation of persistent inflation and expectations of persistent inflation, of our inability to achieve a stable exchange rate system, and of our inability to eliminate disequilibrating capital movements. Despite public utterances to the contrary, the United States and most other industrial nations have not ended inflation and expectations of its continuation. As a result, the managers of their economies hesitate to embark on vigorous antirecessionary or countercyclical policies for fear of quickly returning to serious accelerating inflation. Would the United States Congress or the British Parliament be prepared deliberately to increase their budgetary deficits in the near future to fight recessions? Would monetary policy be sufficiently relaxed to achieve low real interest rates while the dollar remains vulnerable to further depreciation and devaluation feeds the fires of inflation? The myth that we are in a noninflationary period will catch up with the reality of persistent inflation.

Thus, the outlook for the world economy in 1989-1991 is not good. I believe that the U.S. economy *in 1988*, however, will perform at better than a recession rate.

Needed: A Renaissance of the International Monetary System

The significance of this rather gloomy forecast cannot be judged if it is seen as merely a prediction of another downturn in the perpetual roller coaster we call the business cycle. We are now near the end of the second decade of major structural changes in the world economy and finance. It has been an era of repeated surprises, shocks, instability, troubles, and adversities in a world made truly global by worldwide production, distribution, finance, communication, and transportation. There are no insular countries or regions. Vulnerability is universal. The 1970s and 1980s have seen the following unfavorable events and trends:

- Two severe recessions.
- The end of the era of satisfactory growth in world output and trade.
- Massive instability in exchange rates.
- Day-to-day disorder and unpredictability in foreign exchange markets.
- The worldwide stock exchange collapses of October 1987.

- Slow, weak adjustments domestically and externally to major changes in national policies.
- The difficulties and reluctance of governments to pursue fiscal policies needed for satisfactory sustained growth.
- Stubborn consumerism and consequent inadequate savings.
- Continuous speculative fever engendered by persistent inflation as inflation rates are brought down but expectations of inflation continue.
- Continued search for nonproductive investments as inflation hedges and protection against currency devaluations.
- Chronic external debt problems of developing countries.

There have also been major gains in the world economy, but the atmosphere is one of gloom and anxiety. Dissatisfaction with existing conditions is nearly universal. We cannot escape from the reality that this gloom in economic and financial matters is heightened by worldwide fears of AIDS, drugs, terrorism, civil violence, and painful adjustments to unprecedented huge changes in world demographics, population, migration, and urbanization.

There is a worldwide longing for stability, growth, predictability, and certainty--not in any absolute, fixed sense, but reasonable and moderate. Deliberations on the international financial system are part of the worldwide quest for improvement. Unless the international monetary system is able to provide the framework for economic growth, the expansion of world trade, and orderly structural change in output and distribution, we cannot achieve the end of this era of troubles and gloom.

In 1971 the United States brought to an end the existing international monetary system, which until then had been based on the convertibility of the U.S. dollar into gold at a fixed price--the so-called Bretton Woods system. The intent of the agreement made at the conference in Bretton Woods, New Hampshire, in July 1944 was to devise a system of exchange rates at internationally agreed levels to deal with international monetary and financial problems by achieving stability in exchange rates. Exchange rates of currencies were expressed in terms of the U.S. dollar and its gold equivalent, and the price of gold was fixed at $35 per ounce. The United States repeatedly affirmed that this price would not be changed, although exchange rates could be, and were, changed. The rates were changed infrequently in the case of the currencies of the major industrial countries; more frequently in the case of the currencies of developing countries. Currencies were essentially changeable (salable) for each other.

The U.S. dollar was the pivotal currency, the hub in the wheel of the global monetary system. The essential aims of the Bretton Woods agreements were to have an international monetary system that provided the benefits of stable exchange rates and currency convertibility--conditions that were deemed most helpful, even essential, for the efficient conduct and expansion of international trade and productive capital flows. The system was flexible in that it provided for changes in exchange rates agreeable to the international community and even for the use of direct, governmental controls over international payments (if otherwise unavoidable), again with the agreement of the international community. Thus, the flexibility that contained the seeds of uncertainty and unpredictability was tempered by the need to obtain international agreement to any change.

The Bretton Woods system functioned reasonably well. It provided the monetary framework for an unprecedented period of expansion in international trade, world output, and income. The system foundered on the shoals of global inflation, compounded by the huge oil price increases and the recession of 1974-1975. Countries were eager to bring inflation under control, but they did not pursue the needed mix of monetary, fiscal, and income policies. Instead, they relied heavily on monetary policies alone--such as efforts to control the money supply, interest rates, and exchange rates. The United States, like other countries, was caught in the trap of persistent, accelerating inflation. The U.S. dollar, free of any restrictions in its international payments, faced repeated disequilibrating capital movements in what, in certain periods, appeared to be a riskless speculation that the dollar would soon be devalued. At the same time,

U.S. liabilities to foreign monetary authorities--their international monetary reserves and liquidity--rapidly increased after the 1960s and greatly exceeded the available gold stock. With the expectations of further dollar devaluations, central banks could have been expected to convert their dollar holdings into gold at the bargain price of $35 per ounce, but the U.S. gold stock was too small to serve this purpose. The commitment to convert into gold was recognized as hollow. Facts dominated fiction. The link to gold was broken when the U.S. authorities did not choose the alternative of a very large increase in the price of gold (i.e., a huge devaluation in terms of gold). The U.S. action soon ushered in the period of floating exchange rates that still prevails.

International finance has been in a literally shocking phase. Given the present troubled global conditions and the outlook for world recession, there must be an international financial system that remains viable even under severely adverse economic conditions. The present system is not adequate, and it will not be adequate until the following circumstances prevail:

- There is sufficient liquidity available to developing countries to achieve sustained growth based on realistic exchange rates and competitive foreign exchange and trade policies.
- There are stable exchange rates of the major currencies.
- There is a reversal of current trends toward protectionism.
- There are higher rates of growth in the industrial countries.

Also, because any international financial system will experience repeated shocks and surprises, the system needs adequate defenses in place to avoid exchange rate instability, protectionism, and severe restriction on imports by the developing countries. The present defenses are glaringly unsatisfactory, and this inadequacy adds to the prevailing gloom and pessimism.

In achieving the conditions just listed, the overhang of external debt of developing countries must be removed. The overhang of sterling liabilities after World War II undermined the international role of the pound sterling. Fortunately, the external debts of the developing countries are not a direct threat to the international monetary system or to the international role of the dollar, although they are threatening to some commercial banks. The debt situation, however, is crippling and constraining for the entire system as well as difficult for the debtor countries. Many schemes are being put forward for reducing the debt servicing burden. I disagree with most of these schemes because they result in destroying for years to come the creditworthiness of the developing countries. They institutionalize the loss of confidence in the future of these countries.

The debt problem should be handled as part of the global need for expanding economies--that is, for a set of measures that would greatly strengthen the international financial defenses of the world economy and enable us again to enter an era of sustained growth and prosperity. I have urged, as mentioned earlier, very large increases in the financial capabilities of the World Bank, the regional development banks, and the International Monetary Fund, and an effective alliance of these institutions. From my past experience, I know that these objectives are difficult to achieve but that they can be reached. We are moving in the directions of a larger International Monetary Fund, a larger World Bank, more collaboration, and so on. We continue, however, to move too slowly and too little to accomplish what we need and could do.

When we have strengthened our global financial defenses, we can grapple successfully with the restoration of creditworthiness of developing countries with private sources of finance and with attracting private international equity flows. Developing countries in all regions are reassessing and changing their economic management. This is happening, for example, in China and India, which alone account for nearly half of the human race. Everywhere, however, efforts are distorted and failure experienced because the global environment is seen as continuously unfavorable or vulnerable, and the international economic defenses are inadequate. In the altered global environment that I advocate, we can hope to alter the behavior of the private industrialists, traders, and financiers. Hitherto, we have tended to do things backward; we have tried to change the behavior of the actors rather than changing the play. We can, as I have suggested in earlier years, do more to make use of capital market instruments by developing countries. We can make bank assets more marketable. We can have debt-for-equity swaps. But we cannot expect these means to succeed extensively until there is more confidence in the entire system. Mexico cannot restore its creditworthiness by honoring its debts after they have been sold or converted at hugh discounts with resulting huge losses to the original creditors. When the international financial environment is strengthened, some external debt will be sold. But if bank loans are sold at discounts, those discounts will be such that they will not destroy the international financial standing of the borrower. Mexico's past debt will then sell at acceptable premiums or discounts as market conditions change but only when confidence is restored in holding Mexican assets in any form. The public debt of the United States is traded all the time. It falls and rises in price but not in such measure as to destroy public willingness to hold the public debt and thus to destroy the markets for the public debt. We can urge and insist on good economic management by debtor countries if they are to benefit from the strengthened international financial defenses. We can help them on an ad hoc basis as needs arise. We can have temporary successes, but the fundamental adverse conditions will not change until the entire international system is adequately reformed and fortified and the world economy is again on a secular high-growth path.

Under the changed and improved global economic defenses, the external debt becomes manageable. Official debt can be refinanced at long-term rates, or it can even be forgiven without loss of creditworthiness if creditor governments so decide. Some of the private debt will then no longer be regarded as unwanted by the private creditors. The remaining unwanted debt should be refunded on the longest terms possible. A number of years ago I suggested a term of 10 years or more for the commercial banks. It was a bold idea then; it is no longer. Can we have 20 years' rescheduling with five-year grace periods for amortization, market interest rates, continuous interest payments that are automatically capitalized if creditor and debtor agree that contracted servicing is difficult, or unless creditor and debtor have worked out different arrangements in advance, such as accepting payments in local currency debt indexed against inflation and/or exchange rate devaluation? We can have a privately owned special institution to invest in these restructured debt instruments and create markets for investors in such paper. I have advocated a privately owned institution because it would have the means and incentives to do this. Governments should focus on building an adequate international financial system and not confuse the external debt issue with charges of bailouts of private banks. The punishment for a bank in making poor judgments about its lending activities is the need to cope with nonperforming loans or to restructure on feasible terms for the borrower. The basic aim of the unhappy lender is to reestablish the creditworthiness of the borrower. In the meantime, the bank's auditors, controllers, and managers must take steps to protect the bank's financial viability--the interests of depositors and shareholders who need to be protected but not beyond expectations and commitments. Bank supervisors and creditors are there to protect the public interest. Major steps have been taken along these lines, and they have been helpful. If the governments create an adequate defense for the international financial system, the private system can operate efficiently and effectively in this most uncertain, volatile, unpredictable, and dangerous world.

In the meantime, the private banks can take other steps to strengthen the system without government action. As an example, major banks can enter into agreements to continue their interbank lines during periods of crises and danger. These interbank lines are the hard core of the international financial system. Only the leading banks are needed to form this core, which could include only banks that are completely acceptable to the others. It could strengthen the confidence that crises need not paralyze the international financial system because of uncertainty regarding the actions of the major private banks. Crises create hysteria. Hysteria creates overreactions. The major banks can agree in advance to do what they could otherwise do anyway, which is to cooperate with each other in times of stress, avoid crisis situations, and thus avoid hysteria and overreactions by agreeing to maintain their interbank lines.

Another possible step for private lenders is to establish a mechanism for leaders of such major banks to meet and exchange views on the global situation. Such meetings would be similar to the central bank meetings of the Bank for International Settlements (BIS). I am not suggesting another monetary conference but rather quiet, informal meetings without guests, speakers, or addresses. Many "surprising" events are events that might have been anticipated with adequate knowledge--knowledge already known to some but not others. The information needed is not about business activities but views about countries, the world, major industries, technology, and so on. The International Finance Institute in Washington is helpful in improving knowledge of banks and bankers. Also helpful are the close relations of banks with the International Monetary Fund, the World Bank, the Bank for International Settlements, the Export-Import Bank, OPIC, and others. These, however, are not substitutes for informal meetings of peer groups of top managers. The Interim Committee of the Governors of the International Monetary Fund find it useful to meet every six months to exchange views despite the huge volume of work done by the International Monetary Fund staff and executive directors in the intervals. There are many other analogies.

These suggestions are given to encourage more thought on how the private banks can help to improve the functioning of the international system as part of the mixed public and private international financial system.

This volume examines many different facets of international finance. We can all agree that these distinguishable facets are important and interrelated. We need not, however, labor as in past years on now widely recognized phenomena and trends, such as the emerging globalization of world finance and the interdependence of the national economies that make up our world economy. We have also come a long way in understanding that simplistic theories and heroic assumptions lead seductively to seemingly attractive solutions for our various problems, but these simplistic solutions fall far short of providing satisfactory answers in our complex and dynamic world. Perhaps we are also becoming more realistic and sophisticated with respect to the fads and fashions in economic and financial thinking that have hampered and often misled us in the past. Many have come to reconsider their views on monetary policies and to give up the attractive simplicity of believing that changes in the money supply account for changes in the real economy. Others have had to reexamine their views as to the proper roles of various financial institutions in the world economy, needing to relinquish conventional definitions of proper roles and accepting the reality of overlapping and ambiguity. Fiscal theorists have had to reexamine their pet theories about how to fine-tune industrial economies and even their theories on the relationships between fiscal deficits, inflation, and employment.

Exchange rate experts talk less glibly about "J" curves, and with more hesitation they indicate what they believe will be the future course of exchange rates or what would be an equilibrium pattern of exchange rates. Development economists no longer find the answers to the problems of developing countries by focusing on balance of payments and/or savings-investment gaps. Bankers and their analysts are disillusioned with their ability to assess credit, country, and other risks. They seek ways and means to make sensible decisions in a world of uncertainty and risk, or else they fall back on the negativism of withdrawal and inaction. Borrowers no longer assume that banks are the natural and available source of borrowed funds, and investors in capital markets are no longer the most conservative and traditional of lenders and investors. Equity flows are no longer understandable by historical analogies.

These are but a few examples of the intellectual turmoil in which we now find ourselves. Practically every major change in the last few years has resulted in incorrect prognostications about the significance of these changes and about the future. The revaluation of the dollar in the early 1980s, the devaluation in the mid-1980s, the huge U.S. budgetary deficits of the 1980s, the dramatic change in the international capital position of the United States--all resulted in numerous public statements similar to each other in content but all equally incorrect. I see this volume as providing an opportunity to clarify our thinking and to suggest feasible ways and means to improve our ability to cope with the shocks and surprises of tomorrow.

I have not indicated the topics or issues that should be focused on, whether the role of the U.S. dollar, exchange rate policy, interest rates, international financial cooperation, the U.S. balance of payments, the international capital position of the United States, the external debt problems of developing countries, or whatever. I am sure that contributors to this volume and others welcome all ideas and suggestions to improve the international financial system.

CHAPTER 2

ALTERNATIVE OR COMPLEMENTARY ANCHORS FOR THE PAPER-EXCHANGE STANDARD: THE DOLLAR AND ITS MAJOR RIVALS, OR A REFORMED SDR AND THE ECU?

Robert Triffin

Dr. Triffin is best known for his contributions to world monetary reform and regional monetary integration, having played a leading role in the conception and negotiation of the European Monetary System. He has taught at Louvain, Harvard, and Yale, among others. He has served as staff member or consultant with the Board of Governors of the Federal Reserve System, the Council of Economic Advisors, the European Recovery Administration, the International Monetary Fund, the United Nations Economic Commissions for Europe, Latin America, Africa and Asia and the Far East, the European Community, and various central banks in Latin America and elsewhere.

The Evolution of the International Balance Sheet of the United States: 1939-1987

This chapter's background[1] can be summarized in Table 2-1, which is my broadest "guesstimates" of the U.S. international balance sheet.

My "guesstimates" for 1987 are incomplete and provisional. Calculated in mid-February 1988, they could not use the balance-of-payments estimates of the March *Survey of Current Business*. I invite you to complete them and to see how much they differ from those in my table. They lead me to the alarming policy conclusions and forecasts summarized as follows:

1. The richest and most heavily capitalized country in the world, except for a handful of Persian Gulf oil-producing countries, was importing in 1987 about $160 billion from poorer and less adequately capitalized countries--$660 per habitant ($2,500 per household), or more than the total income per head on which some 31/2 billion people of the Third World must survive or starve! This is obviously unacceptable, economically as well as humanely, and in total contradiction with often repeated pious resolutions of the United Nations Assembly, which urges the richer countries to devote at least 1% of their GNP to capital exports to the poorer and less developed countries.

2. Extrapolating the 1987 estimates over the next three years would lead to a forecast of a $1,200 billion *net* indebtedness of the United States to the rest of the world by the end of this decade. Regarded as realistic by some Reagan administration experts and welcomed by them, this forecast seems to me both horrifying and--fortunately--most unlikely to be confirmed by events. Private investors will inevitably reduce (or even reverse?) their capital exports to the United States and make it impossible for central banks to continue their fantastic stabilization interventions of 1987 under the Plaza Hotel, Louvre, Venice, Tokyo, and other "summit meeting" commitments.

Table 2-1: THE INTERNATIONAL BALANCE SHEET OF THE UNITED STATES: 1939-1987 (billions of dollars)

	End of Year							Period Changes		Annual Changes		
	1939	1949	1969	1979	1982	1986	1987	1980-82	1983-87	1980-82	1983-86	1987
I Exchange Market, Net :	+1	-2	+12	-15	-69	-562	-678	-54	-609	-18	-122	-116
A. Gross Assets	11	18	114	441	739	971	1,068	+298	+329	+99	+66	+98
B. Gross Liabilities (-)	-10	-20	-103	-456	-809	-1532	-1746	-353	-938	-118	-188	-214
C. Official and Banks, Net	-3	-5	-31	-120	-15	-240	-318	+105	-303	+35	-61	-78
D. Customers, Net	+4	+3	+42	+105	-54	-322	-360	-159	-306	-53	-61	-38
II Gold and Foreign Aid Assets	18	36	31	194	195	192	215	+1	+31	-	+4	+23
III Net Total (I + II)	+19	+34	+43	+179	+126	-369	-463	-53	-577	-18	-118	-93
Assets	29	54	145	635	934	1163	1284	+299	+360	+100	+70	+121
Liabilities (-)	-10	-20	-102	-456	-809	-1532	-1746	-353	-938	-118	-188	-214

Source: *Survey of Current Business'* latest estimates corrected for the difference between gold valuation at market prices and at irrelevant recorded official prices, and by inclusion of the statistical discrepancy (errors and omissions) as unrecorded capital assets or liabilities.

3. This reduction of capital exports, should, and may at long last, revive the drive for international monetary reform on which an intellectual--if not political--consensus was reached in June 1974 by Jeremy Morse's Committee of Twenty, after 10 years of continuous debates and negotiations of finance ministers, governors of central banks, and their experts, but discarded abruptly in Jamaica and in the second amendment to the IMF Articles of Agreement.

The Obstacles to Overdue International Monetary Reforms

One of the obstacles to these 1974 worldwide reform proposals by the Committee of Twenty has obviously been the reluctance of shortsighted U.S. politicians to abandon the "extravagant privilege" denounced by President de Gaulle: the possibility of financing most of the U.S. deficits through the acceptance of the *national* U.S. currency as an *international* settlements medium by foreign central banks, commercial banks, and other large international investors. This, however, has to be expected: it reduces the need for unpopular tax increases or reductions of expenditures, even if this is contrary to the longer-run national interest.

It would put the major blame, therefore, on the *other* countries for being willing to extend persistently such financing to the United States, for increasingly huge amounts, at the cost of a world inflation without precedent in man's history. But how can this be explained?

First, it can be explained by bureaucratic routine, the negotiating difficulties of agreeing on an alternative world currency to be created *ex nihilo*, and the reluctance of foreign firms in competition with U.S. firms at home or abroad to abandon the advantage derived by them from the resulting overvaluation of the dollar.

Second, the disadvantages of such financing are confined primarily to a few countries with huge surpluses, primarily Japan and Germany. The June 1988 *OECD Economic Outlook* estimates that as much as $131 billion of the U.S. $161 billion 1987 deficit was financed by these two countries: $87 billion by Japan and $44 billion by Germany. Other countries, except the so-called NICs [Newly Industrialized (Asian) Countries], were in deficit or had only moderate surpluses. They felt no strong interest in abandoning their overcompetitiveness vis-a-vis the United States.

The main purpose of this chapter is to find practical ways and means to surmount these obstacles.

Worldwide reforms are, of course, impossible without the active participation of the United States. American economists and public opinion should press their government to alter radically the policies followed so far in this respect under the pressure of shortsighted politicians and vested private interests. These policies are as disastrous for the United States itself as for the rest of the world.

In the meantime, pending such U.S. participation, other countries should do the following:

1. Agree among themselves on the institutional reforms and policy commitments that will minimize, as far as possible, their present overdependence on the vagaries of U.S. monetary and fiscal policies.

2. Facilitate and stimulate U.S. participation by using--as suggested by an old proverb--both the "carrot and the stick."

   a. The "carrot," by couching their own reforms and policies in a manner susceptible of contributing to the solution of the U.S. dollar problem.

   b. The "stick," by denying the United States the "extravagant privilege" of financing the perpetuation of U.S. policies that are prejudicial to all concerned.

The countries of the European Economic Community (EEC) are best able to take the leadership in such regional monetary agreements. The success of the EMS (European Monetary System), which is anchored, theoretically at least, on the European Currency Unit

(ECU) rather than on the dollar or any other national currency, has exceeded all expectations and is now fully recognized by its initial opponents, particularly the Bundesbank of Germany. It must still be strengthened enormously, however, to permit the completion of the fully integrated internal market envisaged for 1992 in the Single European Act signed in February 1986 and ratified by all member countries in 1986 and 1987.

The next section of this chapter summarizes the monetary steps already agreed on in this respect by important political leaders of the EEC. The last section deals with the way in which the success of a strengthened EMS would facilitate the later achievement of the full economic, monetary, and, therefore, political union of the EEC, repeatedly promised by its heads of state and government since the December 1969 meeting in The Hague.

These institutional reforms of the EEC would obviously increase stupendously its role in world economic and political relations, as may be gauged from the following:

1. Its 1987 *gross national product* (about $4,170 billion) was about equal to that of the United States ($4,490 billion) and nearly double that of Japan ($2,340 billion).

2. Its 1987 *population* (323 million) was far larger than that of either the United States or Japan: 245 million for the United States and 122 million for Japan.

3. Its 1986 *exports*, excluding those to other EEC countries ($451 billion), totaled $339 billion. This was over 50% more than those of the United States and 60% more than those of Japan.

Urgent and Feasible: The ECU as a Parallel Currency in External Transactions

Two recent articles of mine concern the use of a reformed ECU, defined no longer as a basket but as a reference currency, not only for central banks but for all external transactions, settlements, and reserve accumulation by the residents of the EEC.[2] These articles answer, I hope, the major political as well as economic objections that have precluded up to now general agreement on the adoption of a truly *international* currency as a practical alternative to the *national* currencies on which was anchored the *gold-exchange standard:* primarily the pound sterling in former days and the U.S. dollar after World War II.

Yet, the international collapse of the pound in September 1931 and of the dollar in 1971 amply demonstrates the ultimate lack of viability of such a system. Professor Kindleberger[3] correctly argues that the dollar has proven more acceptable than the Esperanto but that its management should be entrusted to an enlarged Open-Market Committee, including elected representatives of other countries. Such a proposal seems to me far more utopian than even the most utopian versions of the Triffin plan: No country will ever accept to have its own national currency controlled by foreigners, whereas they will all be not only ready, but determined, to negotiate appropriate controls over the issues of any joint reserve or parallel currency.

The two founding fathers of the European Monetary System and the ECU, Valery Giscard d'Estaing and Helmut Schmidt, formed a committee in 1987 designed to promote such a radical reform and to create the European Central Bank, indispensable to the management of a European reserve currency. A "Coordination Group" of top-level official experts finalized in early 1988 its recommendations in this respect. Comprehensive and detailed agreements have already been reached tentatively on all essential points.

The Bundesbank serves as a model for the autonomy and political independence of the European Central Bank. Its board of directors includes nine members elected by the Council of Ministers from a list submitted to it by the Board of Governors of national central banks.[4] It therefore has a majority representation in an Open-Market Committee of 17 members in which the other eight members are the governors of national central banks: five permanent members are those of the German, French, British, Italian, and Spanish central banks, and three rotating members of those of the other central banks.[3] A Board of Surveillance includes the same national bank governors and, with a consultative voice only, representatives of the Commission of the Communities, the presidency of the Council of Ministers, the Monetary Committee, and the Bank for International Settlements. Finally, the European Central Bank will report periodically its agreed policy objectives to the Council of Ministers and the European Parliament.

The ECU will no longer be a currency basket, varying with every exchange rate realignment, but will be a final "reference currency" vis-a-vis which every member currency's exchange rate will itself be defined. Maximum fluctuation margins will, at first, be brought uniformly to 2.5%, possibly with temporary exceptions for the peseta, the escudo, and the drachma, but reduced gradually to zero. The banks will, moreover, no longer charge any commissions on exchange transactions between the ECU and the national currencies of member countries. Exchange transactions will be costless, as they are already between the member currencies of the French franc area.

Member currencies will therefore be freely convertible at fixed rates among one another and with the ECU, holdings and borrowings in European currencies enabling both the national authorities and those of the EEC to help finance stabilizing market interventions, not only at the agreed margins, as is already the case, but also intramarginally whenever deemed necessary or useful to avoid interventions and repayment in foreign currencies (primarily the dollar today).

Exchange rates vis-a-vis nonmember currencies would, of course, remain variable as long as the return to occasionally readjustable fixed rates, or even the acceptance and implementation of "target zones," remains well beyond the foreseeable horizon. The Committee of Governors of central banks should coordinate the size and direction of official interventions, mostly but not exclusively on the dollar market, by the European and by national central banks, instead of being left excessively, as is the case today, to the discretion of the Bundesbank.

The ECU should be promoted as the main (or sole?) parallel currency of the Community's authorities and residents in the denomination and settlement of international contracts and in banking and financial transactions. As far as the authorities of the Community are concerned, the ECU should replace (a) national currencies in most contracts, receipts, and expenditures and (b) the so-called "green" ECU in the common agricultural policy, through the elimination of the "monetary compensatory amounts." ECU currency notes and bank deposits should be given full liberating power, even for obligations contracted in national currencies. The ECU itself, however, should obviously become the most appropriate unit for European travel checks, international transport fares, postage, and the like. The Bundesbank's overdue acceptance of the ECU as a legitimate currency unit in borrowing contracts will undoubtedly accelerate the spectacular progress of the ECU in banking and financial transactions, particularly if the current drive for the elimination of remaining exchange controls continues in France, Italy, Denmark, and Belgium. I would add, however, two important qualifications in this respect, as follows:

1. Full liberalization of intra-European capital movements will most probably require jointly concerted policies regarding speculative capital movements between Europe and the United States in order to avoid unbearable tensions between traditionally stronger European currencies, such as the German mark, and weaker currencies, such as the French franc or Italian lira. Such tensions were at the root of the last exchange rate realignment of January 1987, for instance. This realignment was caused by a flurry of capital flows toward

the United States and was unjustified by any deterioration in the current account balance or purchasing power parity of the French franc.

2. Even purely intra-European capital movements may at times be considered damaging by the recipient country, where it may create inflationary pressures, as well as by the capital exporting country, where it may create deflationary pressures. *Jointly* agreed and implemented controls could, in this case, be far more efficacious than controls by the latter country only.

These ambitious proposals of the Coordination Group demand appropriate controls over the issue of official and private ECUs. The group envisages that currency notes can be issued more easily through the intermediary of the national central banks or of consortia of commercial banks, but with a 100% reserve requirement similar to that uniting Scottish banks to the Bank of England. Similarly, ECU deposits in commercial banks are subject to a 100% reserve requirement, either directly with the European Central Bank or indirectly through their national central bank.

The European Central Bank will, therefore, be in full control of ECU issues, whose volume will be determined by its own loans and investments and adjusted to the currency needs of an optimal, feasible rate of noninflationary economic growth (about 5%?). It will also control the regional distribution of its portfolio between member countries and nonmember countries, particularly the United States.

The presumptive *global* ceiling on the growth of ECU issues might have to be exceeded at times, in the event of "acts of God" (*force majeure*, in French), such as the two explosions of oil prices. This will require a qualified majority of votes of two-thirds, or even more, depending on the size of the excess regarded as necessary.

Those who equate wisdom with skepticism will, of course, dismiss as utopian the ambitious proposals just summarized. They will point out, rightly, that Ministers of Finance and governors of central banks are prone to advocate, when out of office, the fundamental reforms that they consider as infeasible when in office.

You may be more interested, therefore, in the treaty concluded on January 20, 1988, between the governments now in power in France and Germany, on the twenty-fifth anniversary of the Franco-German treaty signed in 1963 by President de Gaulle and Chancellor Adenauer. President Mitterand and Chancellor Kohl paraphed solemnly, in company with about 20 of their ministers, two additional protocols, soon to be ratified by their Parliaments and creating a Defense and Security Council and an Economic and Financial Council. An important task of the latter will be to assure a closer coordination of monetary policy between the two countries than that already in effect today, enabling them to accept and promote the creation of a European Central Bank. The presidents of the Bank of France and of the Bundesbank, and the French and German Ministers of Finance and Ministers for Economics will make up this council.

The president of the Bundesbank, Dr. Otto Pohl, expressed the agreement of the bank's council but noted that "since the council is to be established in the context of a treaty that is binding under international law and an examination of the legal position was not possible in the brief period of time given to the Central Bank Council to make its decision, the agreement of the Central Bank Council is given with the reservation that the supplementary protocol does not affect the content of Sections 3 and 6 (1) and 12, sentence 2, Bundesbank Act. The Bundesbank requests the Federal Government to communicate this decision also to the French partner to the Treaty and to take it into account when ratifying the Treaty." He explained that this meant "that the freedom of decision and the independence of the Bundesbank in monetary policy affairs must not be restricted," and he answered some critical remarks of Prime Minister Chirac about the Bundesbank's policies.

It is well known that the Bundesbank's authorities have been radically divided about the creation and development of the European Monetary System, of which its former president, Dr. Emminger, was adamantly opposed, as is today its vice president, Dr. Schlessinger. Dr. Pohl, recently reappointed president for a term of eight years, undoubtedly shares the German fears about "premature" commitments to the EMS, and particularly to full monetary union, until the primary objective of price stability, as well as exchange rate stability, can be implemented by a better coordination of national monetary and fiscal policies and guaranteed by the independence of a European Central Bank and its federated national central banks from undue political pressures.

Yet, Dr. Pohl reiterates relentlessly and indefatigably in all his speeches that the ultimate goal of full economic and monetary union, including the merging of all national currencies into a single European currency, under a European Central Bank, must be kept in mind in the formulation of immediately feasible policies. The Basle central banks' agreement, ratified by the Nyborg European Council, indicates that his views are now prevailing within the Bundesbank itself, and most commentators agree that the agreement is working even better than initially hoped for by its proponents.

The European Parliament has also expressed repeatedly, under the leadership of Lord Plumb, Otmar Franz, and Fernand Herman particularly, its strong support for the measures leading to full economic and monetary union of the EEC.

Equally encouraging is the totally unexpected success of the last Brussels Summit of February 1988 regarding the financing of an increased EEC budget, the doubling of subsidies to its poorest members, and the initiation at least of overdue radical reforms of the Common Agricultural Policy.

The *Parachevement* of the Economic and Monetary Union of the United States of Europe?

The completion (*parachevement* in French) of the Economic and Monetary Union, repeatedly promised by heads of states and governments since their first summit meeting at The Hague in December 1969, and of the United States of Europe, aimed for by the greatest European statesmen formally led by Monnet, de Gasperi, Spaak, and others, is still distant and uncertain.

The path toward the first is outlined in my two 1987 papers, referred to previously. I shall summarize them briefly in conclusion. The EMS has altered radically in this respect the transitory provisions of the 1970 Werner Plan, which envisaged first the *gradual* elimination of exchange margins and exchange rate fluctuations, before the *sudden* substitution of the ECU for the national currencies *at the end* of the process only. The EMS, on the contrary, *began* with the creation and development of the ECU as a parallel currency for external transactions, as described in the previous section of this paper. Its success will transform into ECUs the equivalent of well over $1 trillion of bank loans (and deposits) and of securities now denominated in so-called Euro-currencies or Xeno-currencies. The achievement of the monetary union will then merely require the gradual extension of the use of the ECU in domestic as well as external transactions throughout the EEC. This can be done at a different pace in the various countries and is likely to proceed faster in Luxembourg, Belgium, and Italy for instance, and even in Austria (which has recently indicated its desire to join the EEC) than in the United Kingdom or Germany.

As an inveterate optimist, I hope to live long enough to see the end of this venture!

Table 2-2: THE WORLD NETWORK OF BALANCES OF PAYMENTS ON CURRENT ACCOUNT: 1983-1987 (billions of dollars)

Year	1983	1984	1985	1986	1987	Total
United States	-46	-107	-116	-141	-161	-571
Rest of World	+46	+107	+116	+141	+161	+571
A. Industrial countries:	+24	+45	+62	+119	+108	+358
Japan	+21	+35	+49	+86	+87	+278
Germany	+4	+8	+16	+38	+44	+110
Others	-1	+2	-3	-5	-23	-30
B. USSR and Eastern countries	+11	+12	+6	+9	+8	+46
C. Nonindustrial countries	+11	+50	+48	+13	+45	+167
1. OPEC	-22	-7	+4	-28	-4	-57
2. Others	+33	+57	+44	+41	+49	+224
reported	(-37)	(-23)	(-25)	(-9)	(+8)	(-86)
Statistical discrepancy	(+70)	(+80)	(+69)	(+50)	(+41)	(+310)

Source: *OECD Economic Outlook*, June 1988, Table 63, p. 152; and p. 80, 87, and 93.

Note: Line C2 estimates are derived *residually* from "zero totals" for the world, therefore being equal to the sum of the estimates and statistical discrepancy (with reverse sign) reported by the OECD. For further explanations and qualifications, see my article on "The Paper-Exchange Standard: 1971-??," in Paul A. Volcker *et al.*: *International Monetary Cooperation: Essays in Honor of Henry C. Wallich (Essays in International Finance,* no. 169, December 1987, Princeton, NJ), p. 72-73, and particularly footnote (a) of Table I, on page 73.

Table 2-3: INTERNATIONAL BALANCE SHEET OF THE UNITED STATES: 1969-1987 (billions of dollars)

	End of Year				Total Changes			Average Yearly Change			
I Exchange Market	1969	1979	1982	1987	1970-79	1980-82	1983-87	1970-79	1980-82	1983-87	1987
A. Liabilities (-)	-103	-456	-809	-1,746	-353	-353	-938	-35	-118	-188	-214
1. Official	-19	-160	-189	-283	-141	-29	-94	-14	-10	-19	-41
2. Banks	-30	-125	-254	-618	-95	-130	-364	-9	-43	-73	-75
3. Customers	-54	-171	-366	-845	-117	-194	-480	-12	-65	-96	-98
a) Statistical Discrepancy	(-3)	(-39)	(-121)	(-210)	(-36)	(-81)	(-90)	(-4)	(-27)	(-18)	(-18)
b) Recorded	(-51)	(-132)	(-245)	(-635)	(-81)	(-113)	(-390)	(-8)	(-38)	(-78)	(-79)
B. Assets	114	441	739	1,068	+327	+298	+329	+33	+99	+66	+98
1. Official	5	8	23	35	+3	+15	+12	-	+5	+2	-3
2. Banks	13	157	405	548	+144	+248	+143	+14	+83	+29	+41
3. Customers	96	276	312	486	+180	+36	+174	+18	+12	+35	+60
C. Net Assets	+12	-15	-69	-678	-26	-55	-609	-3	-18	-122	-116
1. Official	-14	-152	-166	-248	-138	-14	-82	-14	-5	-16	-44
2. Banks	-17	+32	+151	-70	+49	+118	-221	+5	+39	-44	-34
3. Customers	+42	+105	-54	-360	+63	-159	-306	+6	-53	-61	-38
II Gold and Foreign Aid	42	194	195	215	+152	+1	+20	+15	-	+4	+23
1. Gold, at market price	12	135	121	127	+124	-15	+6	+12	-5	+1	+25
2. Net Foreign Aid Claims	30	58	75	88	+28	+16	+14	-28	+5	+3	-1
III Total, Net (= IC + II)	+54	+179	+126	-463	+126	-53	-588	+13	-18	-118	-93
1. Assets (= IB + II)	156	635	934	1,284	+479	+300	+349	+48	+100	+70	+121
2. Liabilities (= IA)	-103	-456	-809	-1,746	-353	-353	-938	-35	-118	-188	-214
Memo : IV Net Assets reported in Survey Tables	+57	+94	+137	-368	+38	+42	-505	+4	+14	-101	-99
Difference : III - IV = 1 + 2	-3	+85	-11	-94	+88	-95	-83	+9	-32	-17	+6
1. Unrecorded Gold Appreciation	-	+124	+109	+116	+124	-15	+8	+12	-5	+2	+25
2. Statistical Discrepancy	-3	-39	-121	-210	-36	-81	-90	-4	-27	-18	-18

Sources:

1. "International Investment Position of the United States," Table 2 of *Survey of Current Business*, June 1988, and corresponding table in previous issues;
2. *Plus* corrections:
   a) unrecorded appreciation of official gold holdings at market price (amounting at the end of 1987 to 11.5 times their irrelevant official valuation at the latest official price of $42.223 per ounce reflecting its 10% devaluation (from $38 per ounce) on February 12, 1973;
   b) the "statistical discrepancy" (errors and omissions) repeatedly ascribed in the text of accompanying

articles of the *Survey* (and of the *Federal Reserve Bulletin*) is probably due mainly to unrecorded capital transactions, and included as such until 1900 in official U.S. estimates.

Notes:

1. Exchange Market estimates are designed to show *capital* assets and liabilities and exclude therefore:
   a) gold holdings, shown on line II, 1; and,
   b) foreign aid claims, shown on line II, 2, because they could not be used to defend dollar exchange rates on world markets since they are 99% *long-term* assets and more akin to grants than to loans, being usually rolled over or canceled, but rarely cashed at maturity.
2. Gross liabilities (line I A) are shown first because they are the source of the capital assets (line II B) accumulated by the United States in spite of its growing deficits on current account.
3. Line I A2 estimates include both the liabilities of commercial banks and Treasury securities held abroad by the private sector (mostly by banks). This total, formerly known as "dollar balances," reflects essentially the use of the dollar as a world parallel currency rather than as earning investments.
4. The years 1969, 1979, and 1982 were selected as most indicative of major changes in the evolution of important categories of accounts.

Notes

[1] Robert Triffin, "The Paper-Exchange Standard: 1971-19??," in Paul A. Volcker *et al.*, *International Monetary Cooperation: Essays in Honor of Henry C. Wallich* (*Essays in International Finance*, no. 169, December 1987), p. 70-85.

[2] Robert Triffin, "The IMS (International Monetary System...or Scandal?) and the EMS (European Monetary System)," *Banca Nazionale del Lavoro Quarterly Review*, September 1987, p. 239-263.

[3] Charles P. Kindleberger, *Manias, Panics, and Crashes: A History of Financial Crises*, New York: Basic Books, 1978.

[4] Alternatively, the Board of Directors would be limited to seven members, having the same majority of one in a 13-member Open-Market Committee whose six other members would be the governors of the Bundesbank, the Bank of France, and the Bank of England and, by rotation, those of the other central banks.

CHAPTER 3

A PROPOSAL FOR A NEW AND STABLE INTERNATIONAL CURRENCY

John Winthrop Wright

Mr. Wright, a graduate of Amherst, is chairman and president of Wright Investors' Service, Bridgeport, Connecticut, an investment management and advisory organization specializing in the management of pension and other investment funds. In his long career, Mr. Wright has filled numerous positions in the banking, investment, and industrial communities. He has also been sought as an advisor to various committees of the U.S. Congress. He is the author of numerous articles on investment and economic subjects in leading financial journals and is a frequent speaker on these topics.

The dictionary defines "anarchy" as "political and social disorders due to the absence of government control...as a theory that regards the absence of all direct and coercive government as (ideal)...and as confusion, chaos, disorder."

What better definition could be devised for the historical and present state of international monetary relationships! The progression of anarchy by government was historically a result of the progressive increase in the density of the population to be governed, but as long as the requirements of civilized life could be satisfied within the confines and resources of national boundaries, progress toward international regulation and order has been slow, spotty, and of limited effectiveness.

Today, however, mankind's technological program is, in effect, moving toward erasing these national boundaries by the swiftness and universality of global information, transportation, and communication. There is no question but that the explosive growth of international relationships of all kinds, but particularly of trade, finance, and communications, has already created an unprecedented degree of imbalance in foreign exchange, inflation rates, and trade and payment balances. It is even not too much to say that the progressive deterioration during the last 17 years of the stability of international trade and monetary relationships has as its major root cause the absence of any governing regulatory authority over foreign exchange rates and over the amount of money and credit available to finance world trade and the emerging economies.

There is really nothing new in what I propose. In 1977 in speaking to the Economic Club of Detroit, I noted:

> There is finally beginning to be an awareness of the increasingly imminent danger to the international banking system as a result of the massive short-term liabilities of commercial banks, mostly interest-bearing deposits with maturities of less than one year, deposits that are mostly in dollars due to OPEC nations, or in Eurodollars created by the banks themselves out of thin air and used to make long-term loans, many of them to borrowers with questionable credit, especially the less developed countries (LDCs) and deficit-ridden developed nations. Such loans are nominally very profitable at high

interest rates that cannot possibly be paid except out of the proceeds of still more loans with which to meet ever greater debt service charges.

The awareness of this danger is growing. Major European nations should be willing to join the U.S. in accepting some form of effective international monetary fund credit control. But the leadership is missing. It can be provided only by the United States of America, which, although no longer a remote colossus that can remain unshaken by overseas disturbances, still overwhelmingly dominates Western capitalism. The major nations of the world must act together to control the proliferation of all Xeno-currencies as well as Eurodollars, to limit private bank lending to nations, and to establish an effective international central bank with a noninflationary (or at least a stable) currency as a medium for international deposits, loans, and settlements.

Since these words were written and during the past decade, the world's imbalances have become progressively worse. The wonder is that there is today any order or continuity of values at all despite the mountains of debt and the avalanches of falling security prices we have already experienced. Even 10 years ago no one would have even dreamed of predicting that the world total of dollar-denominated bank deposits (M1, M2, and M3)[1] would almost triple in 10 years from \$1.9 trillion to \$5.2 trillion, or that of today's \$5.2 trillion, 30% (\$1.5 trillion) are dollars that are obligations and have mostly been created by non-U.S. banks--not of or by the United States or its banking system. What is more, there is now another \$659 billion in so-called Xeno-currency-denominated deposit obligations at foreign lending/depository banks.

So, although the number of dollars in the United States and those floating around the world has been increasing at an uncontrolled 11% annual rate, the U.S. Gross National Product (GNP) has grown at only 8.5% per year in nominal terms and only 2.6% in constant dollars after adjustment for inflation.

Why? Because while the world's supply of Eurodollars was rising at a 15% annual rate, the U.S. domestic money supply (M1) was increasing at only about an 8.4% nominal annual rate (2.7% in constant dollars) and was being deliberately reduced by the Federal Reserve Board (the Fed) from more than 20% of GNP 10 years ago to lows of 15% in 1982-1985 (only 17% in 1987) during prior decades. Thus, while world trade was being financed with the rapid and unregulated growth of dollar-denominated non-U.S. bank loans and deposits, the U.S. domestic economy was being progressively and systematically starved for working capital and impoverished by usuriously high interest rates as a result of a misbegotten Fed misconception that U.S. inflation was caused by (1) a domestic monetary profligacy that simply did not and had not existed, and (2) by the Fed's failure to exert effective international leadership in bringing about international control of the explosive growth of Eurodollars, Xeno-currencies, and the ensuing multiple expansion of world commodity and energy prices. During the same period, however, money supply of the other major nations in the world grew at much higher real rates (M3: averaging + 5.7% in Japan, Germany, France, and the United Kingdom, and M1 averaging + 3.7%).[1-3]

During the same 10 years, U.S. inflation averaged 5.8% per year versus a 5.7% average for the other four major nations. The average foreign exchange value of the U.S. dollar versus the other four major nations declined a whopping 20%, however, and the U.S. ratio of exports to imports declined from 82% to 60%. Japan's ratio of exports to imports rose from 113% to 153%, and the other three (Germany, France, and the United Kingdom) did not change significantly.

If you are having some difficulty in making either rhyme or reason of the foregoing, it is simply because there is no poetry in instability and no reason in its structure.

Yet this is a history of what happens when "free enterprise" is permitted to deteriorate and to become, in effect, unregulated anarchy.

Today, the time has come for the sovereign nations of the free world to regulate their international, commercial, and financial affairs on a basis comparable to the regulation of domestic institutions. And first is the regulation of the international money supply by a jointly owned international bank with the power to control the liquidity and soundness of international finance.

Specifically, I propose the following program:

1. An International Treaty Organization for Monetary and Credit

Control should be created into which would be incorporated the International Monetary Fund, the Bank for International Settlements, and the World Bank. Within this framework, the IMF would convert the present Special Drawing Rights (SDRs) into a new Universal International Currency, "International Currency Units"--"ICUs" (perhaps as an evolution of Dr. Triffin's "ECUs"). The new "ICUs" would be made 100% immune from foreign exchange rate fluctuations and devaluations.

2. Each nation would continue to be acknowledged as the unqualified sovereign of its own currency--Germany over marks, France over francs, England over sterling, Japan over the yen, and the United States over dollars. But the "ICUs" would become legal tender for the payment of all government and international obligations. Every bank everywhere in the world that expects to clear its drafts internationally would be permitted, when so authorized by its central bank, to make loans and accept deposits in the new ICU currency subject to the IMF regulations and would be required to establish and maintain with the IMF such reserve deposits as would be required from time to time to control ICU loans and credits and to assure the soundness of such loans and the security of such deposits. All banks would be prohibited from making new loans in any currency other than their own or in ICUs. Existing Eurodollar and Xeno-currency deposits and loans would be gradually liquidated or transformed into ICU denomination. Each nation's domestic banks would be fully subject to the control of that nation's central bank, and no new Eurodollar or Xeno-currency loans could be made.

3. The IMF would exchange ICUs for the national currency of participating nations. Initially the participants would be the Group of Seven in a proportionate, trade-weighted basis at current relative foreign currency exchange valuations up to an agreed-upon initial total, which should be very much larger than the meaningless pittance of $21 billion now allocated to SDRs. Thereafter, adjustments for changes in the group's respective relative market exchange values would be adjusted by debit or credit to the accounts of the respec-

tive central banks of the participating nations. Thus, all outstanding ICUs would always be backed by claims on national central banks and would have an aggregate value in national currencies at current exchange rates, which would be exactly equal to their initial values.

4. The result of such an ICU international currency would be to discourage, although not to prevent, the inflation of national currencies, to attract substantial interest-bearing deposits in ICUs by the surplus nations, and thus to make available low-interest loans to borrowing nations in ICUs, thus effectively recycling the surpluses of foreign exchange holdings into ICUs.

5. At a later stage, non-U.S. central banks would be invited to exchange their excess holdings of U.S. dollars for an IMF new issue of international "Consols" which, like the British Consols, would have no maturity. Such an exchange, as Dr. Robert Triffin has suggested in his Princeton paper, should be welcomed, provided that some sort of exchange guarantee can be provided. An exchange of these excess reserve dollars for ICU-denominated "Consols" would meet this requirement.

6. Also, at a later stage (but sooner, rather than later), it would, in my opinion, be desirable to go a step further and make ICUs inflation-proof by requiring that adjustment for changes in the trade-weighted inflation rates of each participating nation be added to the foreign exchange adjustments applied to each participating nation's IMF account, thus ensuring that the potential devaluation of ICUs resulting from the composite inflation rates of the participating nations be offset by corresponding additions to the reserve deposits at the IMF by the participating nations in their domestic currencies.

Consider the alternatives. This program may be called "bold," "daring," even "revolutionary," but it is really only plain common sense. The important thing is that such a program is desperately needed and needed now--not sometime in the future some years from now. The time is short because the evils of uncontrolled foreign exchange fluctuations and of Eurodollar and Xeno loan and currency expansion are still out of Pandora's box and assuming ever more gigantic proportions. If they are left uncontrolled, the result can only be some kind of international nightmare in the course of which U.S. domestic recovery will certainly not be realized. If, on the other hand, these international forces are brought under rational and responsible control, all of our economies will be able to go forward in a world in which...

- Every nation would absolutely control its own currency and its own inflation rate.

- The world could for the first time have an inflation-proof international currency.

- The present and prospective surpluses of particular nations would be smoothly and fairly recycled.

- An international body would have the resources to finance the growth of the less developed countries and the interim requirements of nations with temporarily deficit international payment balances.

- U.S. currency exchange rates would be freed from the depressing effects of a glut of dollars not made in or controlled by the United States.

- No single nation would be subjected to the burden of being the world's "reserve currency" and every nation would be free of the unwanted importation of inflation resulting from uncontrolled Eurodollars or Xeno-currencies.

Notes

[1] M1 consists of: (1) currency outside the U.S. Treasury, Federal Reserve Banks, and the vaults of depository institutions: (2) traveler's checks of nonbank issuers; (3) demand deposits at all commercial banks other than those due to depository institutions, the U.S. government, and foreign banks and official institutions, less cash items in the process of collection and Federal Reserve float; and (4) other checkable deposits (OCDs), consisting of negotiable order of withdrawal (NOW) and automatic transfer service (ATS) accounts at depository institutions, credit union share draft accounts, and demand deposits at thrift institutions. Seasonally adjusted M1 is calculated by summing currency, traveler's checks, demand deposits, and OCDs, each seasonally adjusted separately.

[2] M2 consists of M1 plus overnight (and continuing contract) RPs (repurchase agreements) issued by all commercial banks and overnight Eurodollars issued to U.S. residents by foreign branches of U.S. banks worldwide, money market deposit accounts (MMDAs), savings and small-denomination time deposits (time deposits--including retail RPs--in amounts of less than $100,000), and balances in both taxable and tax-exempt general purpose and broker-dealer money market mutual funds. Excludes individual retirement account and the U.S. government. Seasonally adjusted M2 is computed by adjusting its non-M1 component as a whole and then adding this result to seasonally adjusted M1.

[3] M3 consists of M2 plus large-denomination time deposits (in amounts of $100,000 or more) and term RP liabilities issued by commercial banks and thrift institutions, term Eurodollars held by U.S. residents at foreign branches of U.S. banks worldwide, and at all banking offices in the United Kingdom and Canada, and balances in both taxable and tax-exempt market funds, and foreign banks and official institutions. Also subtracted is the estimated amount of overnight RPs and Eurodollars held by institution-only money market mutual funds. Seasonally adjusted M3 is obtained by adjusting its non-M2 component as a whole and then adding this result to seasonally adjusted M2.

Figure 3-1: COMPARATIVE FOREIGN EXCHANGE RATES OF THE UNITED STATES DOLLAR

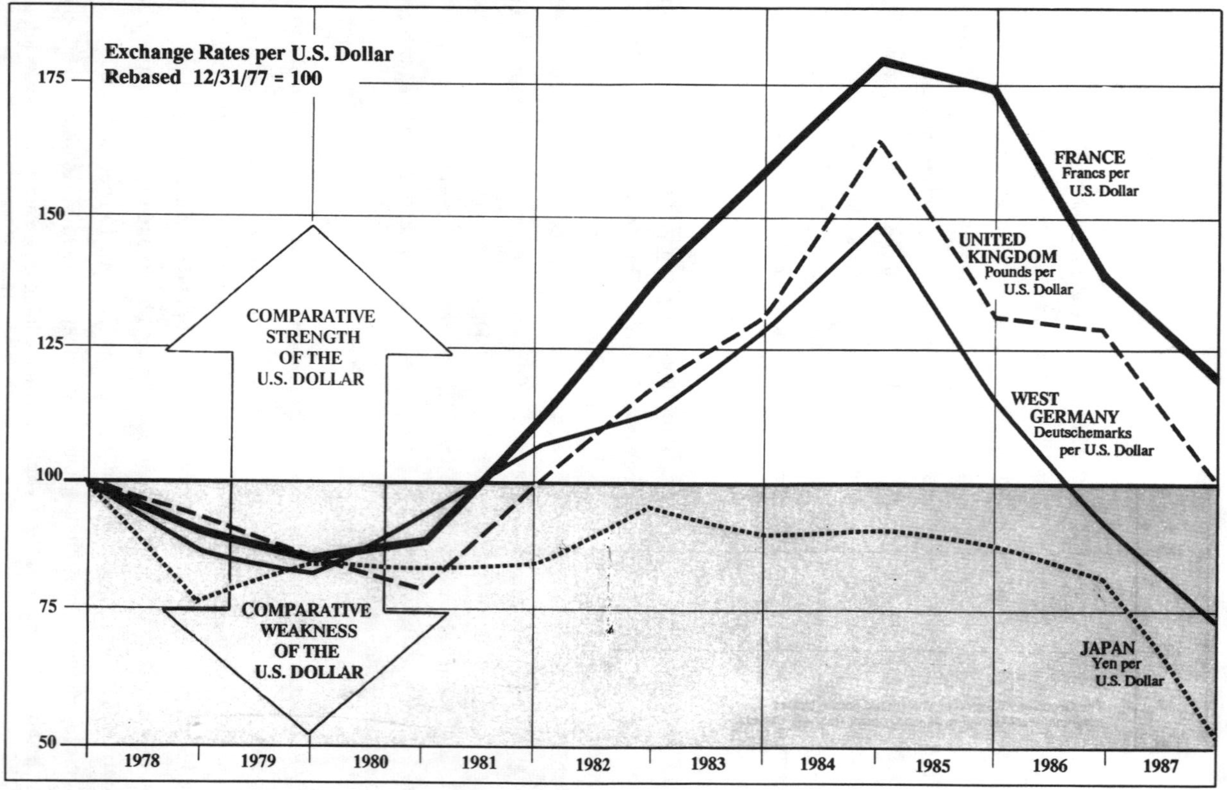

Data prepared by Wright Investors' Service.

Figure 3-2: MONEY SUPPLY (M1) AS A PERCENTAGE OF GNP

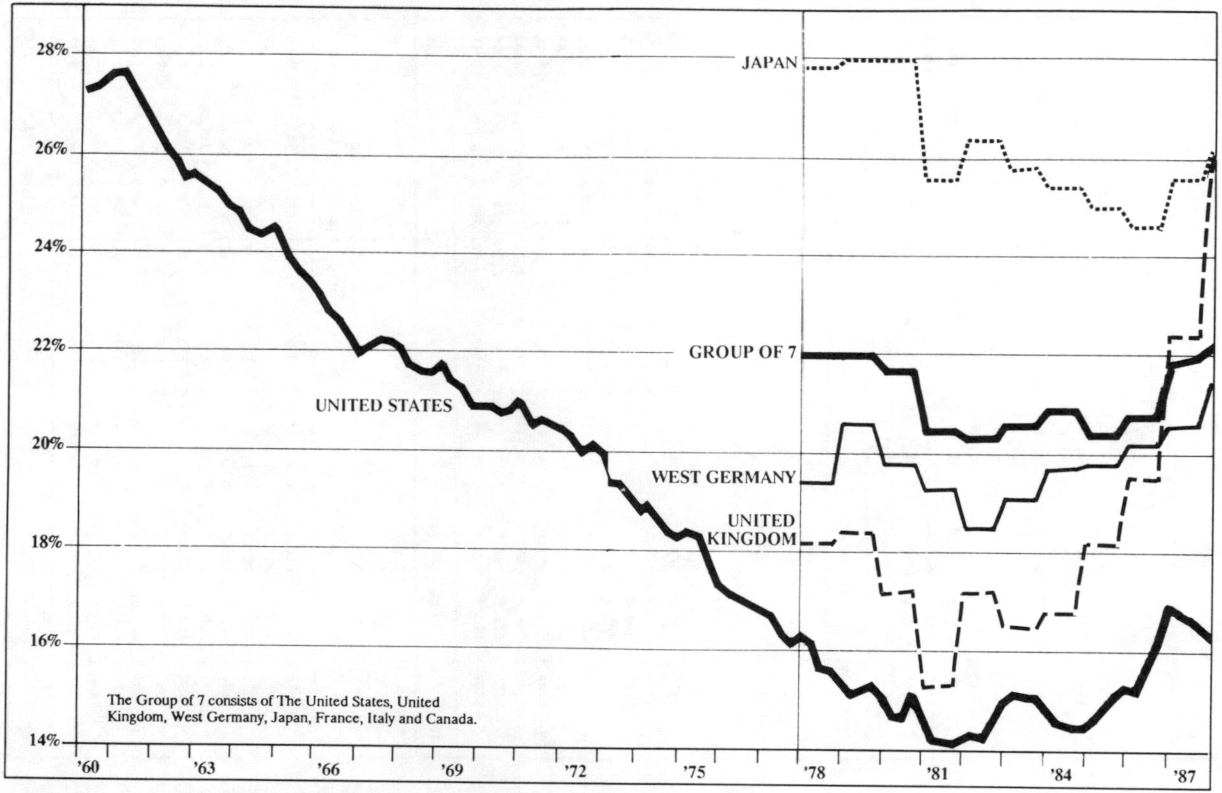

Data prepared by Wright Investors' Service.

Figure 3-3: GROSS NATIONAL PRODUCT

YEARLY AVG. GNP BILLIONS OF $	U.S.			GROUP OF 7 COUNTRIES COMPOSITE			NOTES
	NOMINAL DOLLARS	REAL DOLLARS	REAL % CHG	NOMINAL DOLLARS	REAL DOLLARS	REAL % CHG	
1977	1990.5	3474.8	4.8%	5112.5	8517.9	4.0%	GNP/GDP DEFLATOR IS
1978	2249.7	3659.7	5.3%	5705.3	8910.7	4.6%	REBASED TO 1987=100.
1979	2508.2	3748.8	2.4%	6323.2	9214.9	3.4%	
1980	2732.0	3744.1	-0.1%	6934.1	9338.0	1.3%	COMPOSITE OF GROUP OF 7
1981	3052.6	3817.0	1.9%	7611.5	9496.1	1.7%	ARE TOTALS FOR NOMINAL
1982	3166.0	3717.4	-2.6%	8111.7	9533.5	0.4%	AND REAL GNP/GDP.
1983	3405.7	3851.7	3.6%	8891.0	9814.4	2.9%	
1984	3772.2	4111.8	6.8%	9520.9	10416.4	6.1%	FOREIGN GNP/GDP FOR EACH
1985	4010.3	4236.4	3.0%	10164.0	10715.8	2.9%	YEAR IS SHOWN IN $ VALUE
1986	4235.0	4381.3	2.9%	10755.0	11041.0	3.0%	AT 1987 EXCHANGE RATE.
1987	4488.6	4488.6	2.9%	11255.5	11255.5	1.9%	
10-YR CAR	8.5%	2.6%	-	8.2%	2.8%	-	

YEARLY AVG. GNP BILLIONS OF $	U.K.			WEST GERMANY			JAPAN		
	NOMINAL DOLLARS	REAL DOLLARS	REAL % CHG	NOMINAL DOLLARS	REAL DOLLARS	REAL % CHG	NOMINAL DOLLARS	REAL DOLLARS	REAL % CHG
1977	243.7	560.1	1.2%	682.4	948.8	2.7%	1523.7	1884.5	5.3%
1978	280.2	579.6	3.5%	735.8	981.7	3.5%	1675.3	1980.6	5.1%
1979	327.2	591.5	2.0%	795.9	1021.0	4.0%	1809.0	2084.3	5.2%
1980	382.4	576.5	-2.5%	847.4	1040.4	1.9%	1949.0	2184.3	4.8%
1981	423.4	571.9	-0.8%	880.5	1037.7	-0.3%	2082.6	2271.5	4.0%
1982	464.7	585.6	2.4%	911.0	1024.8	-1.2%	2228.9	2387.4	5.1%
1983	506.6	605.9	3.5%	957.9	1043.6	1.8%	2318.7	2468.3	3.4%
1984	541.0	619.6	2.2%	1009.6	1085.1	4.0%	2466.6	2614.5	5.9%
1985	595.2	645.8	4.2%	1052.3	1106.2	1.9%	2621.9	2691.8	3.0%
1986	634.6	663.2	2.7%	1111.1	1133.3	2.5%	2733.5	2760.8	2.6%
1987	668.2	668.2	0.8%	1137.8	1137.8	0.4%	2856.5	2856.5	3.5%
10-YR CAR	10.6%	1.8%	-	5.2%	1.8%	-	6.5%	4.2%	4.3%

YEARLY AVG. GNP BILLIONS OF $	FRANCE			ITALY			CANADA		
	NOMINAL DOLLARS	REAL DOLLARS	REAL % CHG	NOMINAL DOLLARS	REAL DOLLARS	REAL % CHG	NOMINAL DOLLARS	REAL DOLLARS	REAL % CHG
1977	360.8	830.4	4.4%	149.7	512.8	1.7%	161.7	306.6	2.0%
1978	410.6	864.7	4.1%	175.0	527.1	2.8%	178.7	317.4	3.5%
1979	486.8	888.5	2.7%	212.7	553.2	5.0%	203.4	327.7	3.2%
1980	528.4	885.5	-0.3%	266.7	574.2	3.8%	228.2	330.9	1.0%
1981	595.4	880.7	-0.5%	316.0	575.2	0.2%	260.9	342.0	3.4%
1982	682.2	901.3	2.3%	370.4	573.6	-0.3%	288.4	343.4	0.4%
1983	764.9	923.2	2.4%	425.0	570.4	-0.8%	312.0	351.3	2.3%
1984	821.2	920.6	-0.3%	587.4	688.4	20.7%	342.9	376.5	7.2%
1985	881.0	933.1	1.4%	634.4	707.7	2.8%	366.9	394.7	4.8%
1986	944.3	975.5	4.5%	704.2	737.1	4.2%	392.4	409.6	3.8%
1987	967.9	967.9	-0.8%	721.8	721.8	-2.1%	414.7	414.7	1.2%
10-YR CAR	10.4%	1.5%	-	17.0%	3.5%	-	9.9%	3.1%	3.1%

Figure 3-4: WORLD MONEY SUPPLY

"M1" MONEY SUPPLY IN BILLIONS OF 1987 U.S. DOLLARS

End Of Period	U.S. Nominal Dollars	U.S. Real Dollars	U.S. Real % Chg.	U.S. As a % Of GNP	U.K. Nominal Dollars	U.K. Real Dollars	U.K. Real % Chg.	U.K. As a % Of GNP	West Germany Nominal Dollars	West Germany Real Dollars	West Germany Real % Chg.	West Germany As a % Of GNP	Japan Nominal Dollars	Japan Real Dollars	Japan Real % Chg.	Japan As a % Of GNP	Other Countries in Group of 7 (Canada, France and Italy) Nominal Dollars	Other Real Dollars	Other Real % Chg.	Other As a % Of GNP	Total for Group of 7 Countries Nominal Dollars	Total Real Dollars	Total Real % Chg.	Total As a % Of GNP
1977	335.3	577.7	1.1%	16.8%	44.4	102.3	6.8%	18.2%	132.6	182.6	7.4%	19.4%	423.5	523.1	1.4%	27.8%	188.9	523.4	2.3%	30.3%	1124.7	1909.1	2.4%	22.0%
1978	363.0	579.1	0.3%	16.1%	51.6	107.3	4.8%	18.4%	151.6	200.3	9.7%	20.6%	469.2	553.9	5.9%	28.0%	222.3	559.6	6.9%	31.5%	1257.7	2000.3	4.8%	22.0%
1979	391.1	573.1	−1.0%	15.6%	56.3	102.2	−4.7%	17.2%	157.9	200.7	0.2%	19.8%	506.0	582.0	5.1%	28.0%	260.8	583.5	4.3%	31.6%	1372.2	2041.5	2.1%	21.7%
1980	416.6	555.6	−3.1%	15.2%	58.6	88.7	−13.2%	15.3%	163.9	199.3	−0.7%	19.3%	498.3	557.7	−4.2%	25.6%	284.8	544.6	−6.7%	28.9%	1422.2	1946.0	−4.7%	20.5%
1981	443.2	544.0	−2.1%	14.5%	72.7	98.6	11.1%	17.2%	162.7	189.8	−4.8%	18.5%	548.9	598.1	7.2%	26.4%	316.8	521.7	−4.2%	27.3%	1544.3	1952.2	0.3%	20.3%
1982	481.3	561.8	3.3%	15.2%	76.7	97.0	−1.6%	16.5%	173.9	193.7	2.0%	19.1%	575.9	616.8	3.1%	25.8%	359.1	515.3	−1.2%	26.8%	1667.0	1984.6	1.7%	20.6%
1983	526.9	593.4	5.6%	15.5%	85.3	102.4	5.5%	16.8%	188.5	203.3	5.0%	19.7%	588.2	625.7	1.4%	25.4%	424.4	539.7	4.7%	27.3%	1813.3	2064.5	4.0%	20.9%
1984	557.5	607.1	2.3%	14.8%	98.4	113.2	10.6%	18.2%	200.2	213.0	4.7%	19.8%	616.9	644.0	2.9%	25.0%	472.6	556.6	3.1%	24.8%	1945.6	2133.9	3.4%	20.4%
1985	627.0	662.1	9.1%	15.6%	116.3	126.3	11.5%	19.5%	212.9	221.6	4.1%	20.2%	645.5	663.4	3.0%	24.6%	513.4	563.9	1.3%	24.6%	2115.1	2237.3	4.8%	20.8%
1986	725.4	749.4	13.2%	17.1%	142.0	148.9	18.0%	22.4%	228.5	230.8	4.2%	20.6%	699.5	706.5	6.5%	25.6%	556.4	579.7	2.8%	24.4%	2351.8	2415.4	8.0%	21.9%
1987	750.9	750.9	0.2%	16.7%	174.4	174.4	17.1%	26.1%	245.4	245.4	6.3%	21.6%	747.2	747.2	5.7%	26.2%	564.8	564.8	−2.6%	24.1%	2482.6	2482.6	2.8%	22.1%
10-Yr. Avg.	8.4%	2.7%	–	15.6%	14.7%	5.5%	–	18.8%	6.4%	3.0%	–	19.9%	5.8%	3.6%	–	26.0%	11.6%	0.8%	–	27.1%	8.2%	2.7%	–	21.1%

"M3" = "M1" (MONEY SUPPLY) + QUASI MONEY IN BILLIONS OF 1987 U.S. DOLLARS

End Of Period	Xeno-Currencies Nominal Dollars	Xeno Real Dollars	Xeno Real % Chg.	Xeno As a % Of GNP	U.K. Nominal Dollars	U.K. Real Dollars	U.K. Real % Chg.	U.K. As a % Of GNP	West Germany Nominal Dollars	West Germany Real Dollars	West Germany Real % Chg.	West Germany As a % Of GNP	Japan Nominal Dollars	Japan Real Dollars	Japan Real % Chg.	Japan As a % Of GNP	Other Countries in Group of 7 (Canada, France and Italy) Nominal Dollars	Other Real Dollars	Other Real % Chg.	Other As a % Of GNP	Total Foreign "M3" Nominal Dollars	Total Foreign Real Dollars	Total Foreign Real % Chg.	Total Foreign As a % Of GNP
1977	104.0	190.5		3.3%	93.3	215.0	−3.5%	38.3%	211.4	291.1	7.4%	31.0%	1114.5	1376.7	4.8%	73.1%	410.0	1096.3	3.5%	67.8%	1829.2	2979.2	3.9%	58.6%
1978	142.0	246.1	29.2%	4.1%	107.2	222.7	3.5%	38.2%	239.2	316.1	8.6%	32.5%	1250.4	1476.1	7.2%	74.6%	481.9	1167.7	6.5%	70.5%	2078.6	3182.6	6.8%	60.2%
1979	190.0	316.1	28.4%	5.0%	120.4	218.4	−1.9%	36.8%	259.0	329.1	4.1%	32.5%	1388.6	1597.1	8.2%	76.8%	567.7	1217.0	4.2%	71.0%	2335.6	3361.5	5.6%	61.2%
1980	195.0	304.9	−3.6%	4.6%	142.9	216.5	−0.9%	37.4%	280.7	341.4	3.7%	33.1%	1497.4	1675.8	4.9%	76.8%	624.8	1149.5	−5.5%	66.4%	2545.7	3383.2	0.6%	60.6%
1981	245.0	354.9	16.4%	5.4%	181.9	246.6	13.9%	42.9%	304.6	355.5	4.1%	34.6%	1654.6	1803.0	7.6%	79.4%	689.8	1099.6	−4.3%	63.3%	2830.9	3504.7	3.6%	62.1%
1982	253.0	337.2	−5.0%	5.1%	202.3	255.8	3.7%	43.5%	320.0	356.3	0.2%	35.1%	1784.9	1911.4	6.0%	80.1%	772.1	1080.8	−1.7%	61.6%	3079.3	3604.4	2.8%	62.3%
1983	262.0	323.6	−4.0%	5.0%	224.0	268.8	5.1%	44.2%	328.4	354.3	−0.6%	34.3%	1919.6	2042.1	6.8%	82.8%	996.0	1244.0	15.1%	65.9%	3467.9	3909.2	8.5%	65.6%
1984	261.0	306.0	−5.5%	4.5%	251.9	289.8	7.8%	46.6%	345.5	367.6	3.7%	34.2%	2068.6	2159.5	5.8%	83.9%	1090.7	1270.4	2.1%	60.4%	3756.7	4087.2	4.6%	65.3%
1985	412.0	454.2	48.4%	6.7%	278.8	302.8	4.5%	46.9%	367.7	382.6	4.1%	34.9%	2260.0	2322.5	7.5%	86.2%	1177.0	1285.2	1.2%	59.6%	4083.5	4293.3	5.0%	66.4%
1986	567.0	589.4	29.8%	8.7%	340.2	356.9	17.9%	53.6%	389.2	393.1	2.7%	35.0%	2444.2	2468.7	6.3%	89.4%	1261.5	1313.0	2.2%	59.1%	4435.2	4531.8	5.6%	68.0%
1987	659.0	659.0	11.8%	9.7%	408.4	408.4	14.4%	61.1%	411.3	411.3	4.6%	36.1%	2724.2	2724.2	10.3%	95.4%	1331.1	1331.1	1.4%	60.3%	4874.9	4874.9	7.6%	72.0%
10-Yr. Avg.	20.3%	13.2%	–	5.9%	15.9%	6.8%	–	45.1%	6.9%	3.5%	–	34.2%	9.3%	7.1%	–	82.5%	12.5%	2.0%	–	63.8%	10.3%	5.0%	–	64.4%

TOTAL WORLD MONEY SUPPLY IN BILLIONS OF 1987 U.S. DOLLARS

End Of Period	U.S. "M3" Nominal Dollars	U.S. "M3" Real Dollars	U.S. "M3" Real % Chg.	U.S. "M3" As a % Of GNP	Euro-Dollars Nominal Dollars	Euro-Dollars Real Dollars	Euro-Dollars Real % Chg.	Euro-Dollars As a % Of GNP	Total World Dollar Supply U.S. "M3" + Euro-Dollars Nominal Dollars	Total World Dollar Supply Real Dollars	Total World Dollar Supply Real % Chg.	Total World Dollar Supply As a % Of GNP	Foreign "M3" + Xeno-Currencies Nominal Dollars	Foreign + Xeno Real Dollars	Foreign + Xeno Real % Chg.	Foreign + Xeno As a % Of GNP	Total World Money Supply "M3" + Euro-Currencies Nominal Dollars	Total World Money Supply Real Dollars	Total World Money Supply Real % Chg.	Total World Money Supply As a % Of GNP
1977	1472.9	2537.5	5.1%	74.0%	404.0	696.0		20.3%	1876.9	3233.5		94.3%	1933.2	3169.7		61.9%	3810.1	6403.2		74.5%
1978	1647.1	2627.8	3.6%	73.2%	499.0	796.1	14.4%	22.2%	2146.1	3424.0	5.9%	95.4%	2220.6	3428.7	8.2%	64.3%	4366.7	6852.7	7.0%	76.5%
1979	1806.7	2647.6	0.8%	72.0%	604.0	885.1	11.2%	24.1%	2410.7	3532.7	3.2%	96.1%	2525.6	3677.7	7.3%	66.2%	4936.3	7210.4	5.2%	78.1%
1980	1990.9	2655.3	0.3%	72.9%	761.0	1015.0	14.7%	27.9%	2751.9	3670.2	3.9%	100.7%	2740.7	3688.1	0.3%	65.2%	5492.6	7358.3	2.1%	79.2%
1981	2236.4	2745.2	3.4%	73.3%	910.0	1117.0	10.1%	29.8%	3146.4	3862.2	5.2%	103.1%	3075.9	3859.6	4.7%	67.5%	6222.3	7721.8	4.9%	81.7%
1982	2443.1	2851.5	3.9%	77.2%	1032.0	1204.5	7.8%	32.6%	3475.1	4056.0	5.0%	109.8%	3332.3	3941.6	2.1%	67.4%	6807.4	7997.6	3.6%	83.9%
1983	2692.8	3032.6	6.4%	79.1%	1120.0	1261.3	4.7%	32.9%	3812.8	4293.9	5.9%	112.0%	3729.9	4232.9	7.4%	70.6%	7542.7	8526.8	6.6%	86.8%
1984	2985.7	3251.4	7.2%	79.2%	1169.0	1273.0	0.9%	31.0%	4154.7	4524.4	5.4%	110.1%	4017.7	4393.2	3.8%	69.9%	8172.4	8917.6	4.6%	85.8%
1985	3205.6	3385.3	4.1%	79.9%	1264.0	1334.8	4.9%	31.5%	4469.6	4720.1	4.3%	111.5%	4495.5	4747.5	8.1%	73.1%	8965.1	9467.6	6.2%	88.2%
1986	3491.5	3607.0	6.5%	82.4%	1412.0	1458.7	9.3%	33.3%	4903.5	5065.7	7.3%	115.8%	5002.2	5121.2	7.9%	76.7%	9905.7	10186.9	7.6%	92.1%
1987	3662.4	3682.4	1.5%	81.6%	1511.0	1511.0	3.6%	33.7%	5173.4	5173.4	2.1%	115.3%	5533.9	5533.9	8.1%	81.8%	0707.3	10707.3	5.1%	95.1%
10-Yr. Avg.	9.5%	3.7%	–	77.1%	14.1%	8.1%	–	29.9%	10.7%	4.8%	–	107.0%	11.1%	5.7%	–	70.3%	10.9%	5.3%	–	84.8%

NOTES

GNP/GDP DEFLATOR USED TO COMPUTE REAL DOLLARS IS REBASED TO 1987 = 100.

FOREIGN MONEY SUPPLY IS SHOWN IN $ VALUE FOR EACH YEAR AT 1987 EXCHANGE RATE.

REAL XENO-CURRENCIES ARE DEFLATED BY G-7 INFLATION COMPOSITE EXCLUDING THE U.S.

XENO-CURRENCIES ARE SHOWN AS A % OF G-7 GNP COMPOSITE EXCLUDING THE U.S.

EURO-DOLLARS IS SHOWN AS A % OF U.S. GNP.

Data prepared by Wright Investors' Service.

Figure 3-5: FOREIGN TRADE

RATIO OF EXPORTS (F.O.B.) TO IMPORTS (C.I.F.) IN BILLIONS OF (1987) CURRENT DOLLARS

Yearly Totals	U.S. In U.S. Dollars Exports	Imports	Ratio Of Exp:Imp	JAPAN In U.S. Dollars Exports	Imports	Ratio Of Exp:Imp	GERMANY In U.S. Dollars Exports	Imports	Ratio Of Exp:Imp	FRANCE In U.S. Dollars Exports	Imports	Ratio Of Exp:Imp	U.K. IN U.S. DOLLARS Exports	Imports	Ratio Of Exp:Imp	ITALY IN U.S. DOLLARS Exports	Imports	Ratio Of Exp:Imp	CANADA IN U.S. DOLLARS Exports	Imports	Ratio Of Exp:Imp	GROUP OF 7 COMPOSITE IN U.S. DOLLARS Exports	Imports	Ratio Of Exp:Imp
1977	121.2	147.7	0.82	155.6	137.5	1.13	174.3	149.8	1.16	54.5	56.4	0.97	60.4	68.3	0.88	34.5	36.7	0.94	34.0	32.3	1.05	634.5	628.8	0.99
1978	143.6	172.0	0.83	147.8	120.3	1.23	181.5	155.3	1.17	60.9	60.5	1.01	66.8	74.7	0.89	41.1	41.4	0.99	40.6	38.2	1.08	682.2	662.3	0.97
1979	181.7	206.3	0.88	162.0	174.3	0.93	200.3	186.1	1.08	72.9	74.6	0.98	76.7	88.5	0.87	51.8	55.8	0.93	50.1	47.9	1.04	795.4	833.6	1.05
1980	220.8	257.4	0.86	211.3	230.0	0.92	223.2	217.5	1.03	83.6	93.9	0.89	89.4	93.9	0.95	57.7	73.9	0.78	58.1	52.8	1.10	944.0	1019.5	1.08
1981	233.7	273.3	0.86	240.6	226.2	1.06	252.8	235.2	1.08	98.3	106.9	0.92	95.7	96.6	0.99	74.4	89.6	0.83	63.9	60.6	1.05	1059.4	1088.4	1.03
1982	212.3	254.9	0.83	247.5	234.8	1.05	272.6	239.8	1.14	107.9	123.8	0.87	104.8	107.4	0.98	85.8	100.4	0.85	64.5	51.8	1.25	1095.3	1113.0	1.02
1983	200.5	269.9	0.74	251.0	215.8	1.16	275.4	248.6	1.11	123.2	131.6	0.94	114.2	124.6	0.92	95.5	105.4	0.91	69.1	57.6	1.20	1129.0	1153.5	1.02
1984	218.0	341.2	0.64	289.9	232.3	1.25	311.1	276.7	1.12	145.0	149.2	0.97	133.1	148.3	0.90	111.5	128.1	0.87	85.7	72.8	1.18	1294.3	1348.6	1.04
1985	212.8	352.5	0.60	301.6	223.5	1.35	342.2	295.5	1.16	154.5	159.6	0.97	147.8	159.6	0.93	129.4	149.4	0.87	91.1	80.0	1.14	1379.4	1420.0	1.03
1986	216.6	383.0	0.57	253.7	155.0	1.64	335.3	263.6	1.27	147.2	147.1	1.00	137.9	162.4	0.85	125.6	128.8	0.98	91.9	85.9	1.07	1308.2	1325.8	1.01
1987	252.9	424.1	0.60	239.4	156.2	1.53	335.8	260.9	1.29	151.6	156.9	0.97	150.7	177.5	0.85	143.8	151.4	0.95	95.4	88.5	1.08	1369.6	1415.4	1.03
10-Yr. Avg	201.3	280.2	0.75	227.3	191.4	1.21	264.0	229.9	1.15	109.1	114.6	0.95	107.0	118.4	0.91	86.5	96.4	0.90	67.7	60.8	1.11	1062.9	1091.7	1.02

INFLATION — GNP/GDP IMPLICIT PRICE DEFLATORS

End Of Year	U.S. Index	Yearly % Chg.	JAPAN Index	Yearly % Chg.	GERMANY Index	Yearly % Chg.	FRANCE Index	Yearly % Chg.	U.K. Index	Yearly % Chg	ITALY Index	Yearly % Chg	CANADA Index	Yearly % Chg	GROUP OF 7 COMPOSITE WEIGHTED BY GROSS NATIONAL PRODUCT Index	Yrly % Chg
1977	58.0	6.8%	81.0	5.6%	72.6	3.6%	43.6	9.3%	43.4	13.9%	29.0	18.9%	52.9	7.4%	54.6	6.5%
1978	62.7	8.0%	84.7	4.6%	75.7	4.2%	47.5	9.1%	48.1	11.0%	33.1	13.9%	56.4	6.7%	57.7	5.7%
1979	68.2	8.9%	86.9	2.6%	78.7	4.0%	52.7	10.8%	55.1	14.5%	38.3	15.9%	62.2	10.3%	60.1	4.2%
1980	75.0	9.9%	89.4	2.8%	82.2	4.5%	59.8	13.5%	66.0	19.8%	46.2	20.6%	69.1	11.1%	64.0	6.4%
1981	81.5	8.7%	91.8	2.7%	85.7	4.2%	67.8	13.4%	73.7	11.7%	54.7	18.3%	76.5	10.6%	69.1	7.9%
1982	85.7	5.2%	93.4	1.8%	89.8	4.8%	75.8	11.8%	79.1	7.3%	64.4	17.8%	84.1	10.0%	75.1	8.7%
1983	88.8	3.6%	94.0	0.7%	92.7	3.2%	83.1	9.6%	83.3	5.3%	74.1	15.0%	89.1	5.8%	81.0	7.9%
1984	91.8	3.4%	95.8	1.9%	94.0	1.4%	89.3	7.4%	86.9	4.4%	80.9	9.2%	90.4	1.5%	85.3	5.4%
1985	94.7	3.1%	97.3	1.6%	96.0	2.2%	94.5	5.8%	92.1	5.9%	88.1	8.9%	93.3	3.2%	90.7	6.3%
1986	96.8	2.2%	99.0	1.7%	99.0	3.1%	97.0	2.7%	95.3	3.5%	95.1	8.0%	96.0	2.9%	96.2	6.0%
1987	100.0	3.3%	100.0	1.0%	100.0	1.0%	100.06	3.1%	100.0	4.9%	100.0	5.1%	100.0	4.2%	100.0	4.0%
10-Yr. CAR.		5.6%		2.1%		3.3%		8.7%		8.7%		13.2%		6.6%		6.2%

FOREIGN EXCHANGE VALUE OF THE U.S. DOLLAR

End Of Year	The U.S. $ Trade-Weighted Value Group of 7 Index	% Chg	JAPAN /$	Index	% Chg	WEST GERMANY DM/$	Index	% Chg	FRANCE FRCS/$	Index	% Chg	U.K. /$	Index	% Chg	ITALY LIRA/$	Index	% Chg	CANADA C$/$	Index	% Chg
1977	100.0	−7.5%	261.88	100.0	−11.0%	2.1048	100.0	−10.9%	4.8720	100.0	1.0%	0.5247	100.0	−10.7%	872	100.0	−0.4%	1.0710	100.0	8.9%
1978	87.9	+12.1%	201.95	77.1	−22.9%	1.8278	86.8	−13.2%	4.3928	90.2	−9.8%	0.4915	93.7	−6.3%	830	95.2	−4.8%	1.1558	107.9	7.9%
1979	87.1	−0.9%	221.78	84.7	9.8%	1.7316	82.3	−5.3%	4.1722	85.6	−5.0%	0.4496	85.7	−8.5%	804	92.2	−3.1%	1.1643	108.7	0.7%
1980	91.1	4.6%	219.30	83.7	1.1%	1.9589	93.1	13.1%	4.3125	88.5	3.4%	0.4193	79.9	−6.8%	930	106.7	15.7%	1.1766	109.9	1.1%
1981	104.0	14.2%	222.06	84.8	1.3%	2.2548	107.1	15.1%	5.4780	112.4	27.0%	0.5241	99.9	25.0%	1200	137.7	29.1%	1.1950	111.6	1.6%
1982	116.7	12.2%	250.63	95.7	12.9%	2.3764	112.9	5.4%	6.7177	137.9	22.6%	0.6194	118.1	18.2%	1370	157.1	14.1%	1.2467	116.4	4.3%
1983	127.0	8.8%	236.81	90.4	−5.5%	2.7241	129.4	14.6%	7.7950	160.0	16.0%	0.6894	131.4	11.3%	1658	190.2	21.1%	1.2345	115.3	−1.0%
1984	142.6	12.3%	239.29	91.4	1.1%	3.1476	149.5	15.6%	8.8048	180.7	13.0%	0.8647	164.8	25.4%	1934	221.9	16.6%	1.3086	122.2	6.0%
1985	125.8	−11.8%	227.62	86.8	−4.9%	2.4612	116.9	−21.8%	8.5410	175.3	−3.0%	0.6923	131.9	−19.9%	1678	192.4	−13.3%	1.3734	128.2	5.0%
1986	103.9	−17.4%	163.77	62.5	−28.1%	1.9406	92.2	−21.2%	6.7941	139.4	−20.5%	0.6782	129.3	−2.0%	1359	155.8	−19.0%	1.3882	129.6	1.1%
1987	87.0	−16.2%	139.09	53.1	−15.1%	1.5696	74.6	−19.1%	5.8681	120.4	−13.6%	0.5299	101.0	−21.9%	1157	132.7	−14.8%	1.3111	122.4	−5.6%
10-Yr. CAR.		−1.4%			−6.1%			−2.9%			1.9%			0.1%			2.9%			2.0%

NOTES

FOREIGN TRADE FOR EACH YEAR IS SHOWN IN $ VALUE AT THE 1987 EXCHANGE RATE.

INFLATION INDEX IS REBASED TO DECEMBER 1987 = 100

Data prepared by Wright Investors' Service.

CHAPTER 4

DOLLAR DOMINANCE OR YE$-TROIKA? EUROPE'S ECU: A NEW GEOPOLITIC INSTRUMENT

André A.L. Swings

Mr. Swings, a Belgian citizen and resident, is a graduate of Sint-Ignatius Antwerp. After his military service, he joined the Kredietbank, which he has served in various capacities, including managing the Foreign Division in Luxembourg and the representative office of the Kredietbank Group in New York. In 1970 he returned to Belgium to set up and manage Kredietbank's Marketing Division. In 1973 he returned to the international scene and is now the general manager at Kredietbank's head office, where he is responsible for the bank's Treasury and Foreign Exchange divisions. He is an expert on the European Currency Unit.

"And today, in Frankfurt, West Germany, American tourists were turned down when trying to make a payment with American dollar traveler's checks. Can you imagine?"

This is what I heard, and never will forget, on local radio in my car when traveling in Oklahoma in May 1968. The radio commentator may have known that in West Germany payments are normally made in deutsche marks but took it for granted that West Germany and the rest of the world accept and with pleasure U.S. dollars as well.

Those were the days when Charles de Gaulle, then president of France, dared to make use of a confirmed right to ask for conversion of (part of) France's monetary U.S. dollar reserves into gold. In the Big Apple, some restaurants retaliated by pouring French wine into the gutters before TV cameras. A pity about the wine!

But has the ex-colony come to realize that the world will not be better off by a mere reversal of roles, by replacing one "mother country" by another, by making a former mother country into a new colony, by colonizing the whole world, monetarily too? In other words, is that Oklahoma radio man still typical of this great country, or is there already a growing minority aware of the fact that things are a-changing, monetarily too, in today's world that does not stop at the frontiers of this great country?

Dollar Dominance: Is It Changing?

For several decades now, the U.S. dollar has indeed dominated the world. This is evidenced not only by Americans traveling around the world and making payments with their own greenbacks wherever they find themselves (except in Fidel's Cuba), but also in such world-spanning but U.S.-based institutions as the World Bank and the IMF. That these institutions have shifted from the U.S. dollar to the Special Drawing Right (SDR) should not mislead us. The SDR, being defined as a basket of several currencies, is dominated by its U.S. dollar component, and thus far the Americans have seen to it that its use remains restricted to an absolute (or perhaps obsolete) minimum. Thus, only a visual impression of shifting away from the U.S. dollar, of sharing with other currencies, has been created.

Tables 4-1 and 4-2 show a few key areas in which the dollar dominance is evident, although equally evident is the diminishing degree thereof. The U.S. dollar dominance is evident [even though in the September 1987 figures for external *assets* in domestic currencies, the figure for U.S. dollars is exceptionally smaller (Table 4-3) than that for all other currencies together]. This dominance is even more striking when the two U.S. dollar bank credit lines are taken together (Table 4-4). Also evident, however, is a trend of diminishing U.S. dollar dominance, and this would be even more marked if a longer period were to be taken into consideration.

Table 4-1: CURRENCY COMPOSITION OF MONETARY RESERVES, END OF YEARS 1978 AND 1986 (in percentages)

Currency		1978		1986
US dollar		75.6		49.9
Deutsche mark	11.0		12.1	
Pound sterling	1.7		1.9	
French franc	1.2		1.0	
Dutch guilder	0.9		0.8	
		14.8		15.8
ECU[a]		0.0		12.2[a]
EC subtotal		14.8		28.0
Swiss franc		2.3		1.3
Japanese yen		3.2		5.7
Other		4.1		15.1
		100.0		100.0

Source: IMF-Annual Report 1987 (Table I-3) and IMF-Annual Report 1984 (Table 3).

[a] ECUs issued by the European Monetary Cooperation Fund against both dollars and gold.

Table 4-2: CURRENCY BREAKDOWN OF BANKS REPORTING THEIR EXTERNAL POSITIONS TO THE BANK FOR INTERNATIONAL SETTLEMENTS IN BASLE, SWITZERLAND (in percentages)

	December 1985		September 1987	
	Assets	Liabilities	Assets	Liabilities
Reporting banks in industrial countries				
A. Foreign currencies:				
US dollar	33.5	38.2	31.5	34.9
Others	15.8	16.6	18.0	20.0
Deutsche mark	(6.5)	(6.5)	(6.4)	(7.3)
Pound sterling	(0.9)	(1.1)	(1.2)	(1.5)
French franc	(0.6)	(0.7)	(0.6)	(0.7)
Dutch guilder	(0.4)	(0.5)	(0.4)	(0.5)
Belgian franc	(0.3)	(0.3)	(0.3)	(0.3)
Italian lire	(0.2)	(0.2)	(0.3)	(0.3)
	(8.9)	(9.3)	(9.2)	(10.6)
Swiss franc	(3.2)	(3.6)	(3.0)	(3.8)
Japanese yen	(2.0)	(1.9)	(3.2)	(2.9)
Other currencies	(1.7)	(1.8)	(2.6)	(2.7)
B. ECU	1.5	1.5	1.7	1.5
C. Domestic currencies:				
US dollar	15.6	13.8	11.8	11.9
Others	11.1	8.1	15.2	11.2
D. Total (A+B+C)	77.5	78.2	78.3	79.5
Reporting banks in other countries	22.5	21.8	21.7	20.5
Grand total	100.0	100.0	100.0	100.0

Source: BIS, International Banking Developments, Feb. 1988 (parts of Table 3a were used as a basis for computing these percentages).

Table 4-3: CURRENCY DISTRIBUTION OF EXTERNAL BOND OFFERINGS (in percentages)

	1984	1987
US dollar	57.3	37.7
Deutsche mark	7.8	8.4
Pound sterling	4.9	8.0
French franc	-	1.3
Dutch guilder	2.1	1.2
	14.8	18.9
ECU	3.3	4.1
EC subtotal	18.1	23.0
Swiss franc	14.6	13.0
Japanese yen	7.1	13.9
Australian dollar	0.2	5.1
Canadian dollar	1.7	3.4
Other	1.0	3.7
	100.0	100.0

Source: *OECD-Financial Market Trends*, Feb. 1988.

Table 4-4: CURRENCY DISTRIBUTION OF EXTERNAL BANK LOANS (in percentages)

	1984	1987
US dollar	66.9	66.9
Deutsche mark	2.7	2.2
Pound sterling	4.5	13.4
ECU	3.4	2.3
EC subtotal	10.6	17.9
Swiss franc	2.0	0.7
Japanese yen	16.3	11.0
Other	4.2	3.5
Total	100.0	100.0

Source: *OECD-Financial Market Trends,* Feb. 1988.

Table 4-5: INTERNATIONAL USE OF CURRENCIES (percentages--1979 weights)

	Country's Share in World Exports	Currency's Share in Exports	Cumulative Share of Currencies
US dollar	11.7	14.4	69.2
Pound sterling	5.9	7.5	76.7
French franc	6.3	6.4	83.1
Dutch guilder	4.1	3.0	86.1
Belgian franc	3.6	2.6	88.7
Italian lira	4.7	1.9	90.6
Danish krone	0.9	0.8	91.4
Irish punt	0.5	0.3	91.7
EC subtotal	37.1	36.8	
Swiss franc	1.7	2.1	93.8
Japanese yen	6.6	2.3	96.1
Swedish krone	1.8	1.7	97.8
Austrian schilling	1.0	0.8	98.6
Finnish markka	0.7	0.0	98.6
	48.9	98.6	98.6

U.S. dollar dominance is striking in Tables 4-3 and 4-4, in particular in that for bank loans, where its market share did not drop at all but stayed put at the very high level of 66.9%. Whereas the share of European Economic Community currencies has risen substantially in both tables, it is also striking that the share of the Japanese yen in external bank loans has actually dropped steeply from 16.3% to 11.0%.

From a detailed study by S.A.B. Page published in the *National Institute Economic Review* in November 1981, we took the information given in Table 4-5. With less than 12% of the world exports, about 55% of these global exports are contracted for in U.S. dollars, another dramatic example of U.S. dollar dominance and one of many "public and private international financial imbalances this conference focuses on in the belief that orderly management of international and financial transactions is essential for increasing overall world prosperity, while avoiding economic decline."[1]

Is Anyone to Blame?

One should certainly not blame the Americans, even less so the Americans alone, for this imbalance and concentration in currency use and distribution. The fact is that the United States is a rather vast country (although not much vaster than, for example, Australia, and much smaller than, for example, Canada), endowed with rich natural resources (plus a climate conducive to a wide variety of economic activities), having won with its allies World War II, which it fought on foreign soil (and thus left with its own production base intact), and last but not least, a country that forged its own political union rather quickly more than a century ago, be it at a cost of a Wounded Knee and some other minor injuries. The fact is, too, that Europe, although sharing many of the assets just mentioned for the United States, until many years after World War II stood actively divided, dotting her landscape with monuments for its many hundreds of thousands of great heroes fallen in such places as Waterloo, Verdun, Ypres, Passendale, and other playgrounds of her great statesmen.

Dominance still could be accepted, even defended, if there were no detrimental effects on those dominated. Dollar dominance would be acceptable if the dollar's behavior were commensurate with its predominant presence and in keeping with a perception of responsibility toward all those exposed to that currency. It goes without saying that those exposed cannot be the Americans alone. But it is also evident that to expect responsible behavior toward the whole world dominated by the U.S. dollar, or by any national currency, is asking for the moon.

Is anyone surprised, then, to see the U.S. dollar flickering back and forth, doubling or halving in value, without the U.S. government being seriously worried about it? All the while, the rest of the so-called free Western world, except for those newly industrialized countries and others that have their local currency strongly tied to the U.S. dollar, is continually suffering from this behavior of the dollar. Western we may be, but free? Hence, if being dominated by someone or something else may not necessarily be a problem, being continually exposed to the possible wild swings of the U.S. dollar is a problem indeed. What can we do about it?

Europe's Reply

Sandwiched between the United States of America to the west and a monolithic Japan to the east, Europe's only possible reply, if she is not to succumb, is to pull herself together, to unify--not just as a loosely knit free-trade association, and not merely as a customs union or a more or less intense cooperation of independent nations sticking to their centuries-old traditions. Europe has to integrate economically, industrially, financially, fiscally, monetarily...eventually also politically. It is not necessary to elaborate on all these fields (I certainly would not be able to do so). But I have to expand on the monetary aspects of Europe's monetary integration as an essential ingredient of her political union.

The European Monetary System (EMS) and Its European Currency Unit (ECU)

When the heads of state or government of the then nine member countries of the European Economic Community in December 1978 invented the EMS and its ECU, it was not the first initiative on the road toward European monetary integration and unification, but it probably was the decisive one. Effectively launched in March 1979, the EMS's main purpose was to create a zone (the EEC) of relatively stable foreign exchange rates (i.e., between the EEC currencies themselves). I did not say fixed rates of exchange, but stable, yet adaptable ones, to be adapted from time to time in the light of prevailing circumstances after mutual consultation and with unanimity.

Therefore a grid of bilateral central rates was established between the EEC currencies, and it was agreed that market rates would be kept, if at all possible, within 2.25% above or below the respective central rates, except for the Italian lira, which was granted an exceptional and temporary 6% margin above or below its central rates.

Several short- and medium-term credit lines were established whereby each EEC central bank puts certain credit lines in its respective national currency at the disposal of the other EEC central banks, with which the latter can, whenever necessary, intervene in the foreign exchange markets to keep their own national currency at or near the respective agreed central rates. It is important, however, to note that two EEC currencies have not yet had central rates established for themselves (i.e., sterling and the Greek drachma) and are consequently free-floating currencies.

Since the first grid of bilateral central rates was established, it has been amended 11 times. Sometimes, all the rates were amended; sometimes, only some of them were. In the early years of the EMS these (sometimes general) "realignments" succeeded one another rather rapidly--about twice a year. Over the past five to six years, the pace has slowed down, the latest realignment dating from January 12, 1987, reflecting an increased convergence of the respective policies pursued by the EEC member states and resulting indeed in more stable bilateral exchange rates for these states' respective national currencies.

Here Comes the ECU

Short for European Currency Unit, the ECU was defined by the same European authorities who at the same time created the EMS as a simple basket of, in principle, all EEC currencies. The actual composition was meant to be a more or less true reflection of the respective economic weights of each EEC member country. Three specific criteria were used therefore: (1) each country's relative share in the total volume of the EEC's GNP; (2) intra-European trade, and (3) the EMS's short- and medium-term credit lines referred to earlier.

Thus today, the ECU is composed of 3.71 BEF (about ±8.6% of its total value) plus 0.719 DEM (about ±34.90% of its total value) plus 1.31 FRF (about ±18.8% of its total value), and on and on. In 1979 there were only nine member countries and hence nine component currencies. Today, since Greece has acceded to the EEC and its drachma to the ECU basket, there are 10. The currencies from the youngest EEC member countries, Spain and Portugal, have yet to accede.

Whereas the weight of each ECU component currency varies continuously with the varying valuation of each currency as reflected in the actual foreign exchange rates, the actual number of each component's units in the basket remains fixed, in principle, for five years. Every five years, according to certain procedural rules, the absolute figures of the ECU basket definition are then reviewed in order to bring the relative weight of each component back in line, if necessary, with each country's economic weight in the total EEC.

Again, such actual revision or change of the ECU basket definition requires unanimity among all EEC member countries. And if such a change is decided upon, the new basket's value must initially equal the old basket's value--that is, on the basis of foreign exchange rates prevailing the first day of the new basket's existence.

So far, the ECU's definition has been changed only once, on September 17, 1984. The units of the stronger currencies, DEM and NLG in particular, were reduced, and the units of the weaker currencies, FRF and ITL in particular, were augmented. The next review will normally take place in September 1989, at which time the Spanish peseta is likely to accede as well.

Initially, the ECU was meant to be used as a unit of account in transactions between central banks participating in the EMS. It is interesting to note that exactly the same basket-type unit of account has progressively been used already since 1975 by several European bodies such as the Council (of Ministers), the Commission (the EEC's executive arm), the European Coal and Steel Community, Euratom (European Atomic Energy Authority), the European Investment Bank, and others as a bookkeeping device or unit of account in which to express their budgets and indeed their bookkeeping system. In fact, as far as the ECU proper is concerned, nothing but its name was invented in December 1978.

But the importance of that simple name--the European Currency Unit--for that simple basket, officially created by the highest European authorities, was to be of paramount psychological and political importance. It was the expression of the hope and the will to work pragmatically toward European monetary integration, toward a united Europe that monetarily would have its own identity, a truly European currency to be issued and controlled by a truly European Central Bank (System).

The start was modest enough. As far as the EMS proper was concerned, the short- and medium-term credit lines that were reciprocally arranged by the participating central banks were expressed in ECUs. And the European Monetary Cooperation Fund entered into quarterly swaps with these central banks, crediting them in its books with ECUs created against 20% of their gold and U.S. dollar reserves. These official ECUs represented in September 1987, as indicated in Table 4-1, 12.2% of global monetary reserves, ranking second after the 49.9% of the U.S. dollar but before the 12.1% of the deutsche mark.

Is that all? Yes, more or less, as far as the official ECU is concerned. But it is against the backdrop of an officially created, supported, and promoted EMS and ECU that a rapidly growing and diversified ECU market could develop and, indeed, has developed.

The Private ECU Market

The private ECU market developed quickly, helped by a formal or de facto recognition as a foreign currency in all but one of the EEC member countries. In the Federal Republic of Germany it is not recognized as a foreign currency, but since June 1987 one has been free to use it anyway. Also, the inclusion of the ECU in the list of foreign currencies to be daily and officially fixed (in Rome, Milan, Paris, Brussels, Copenhagen, Lisbon, Amsterdam, Madrid, and so on) was a boost.

In January through September 1987, the ECU ranked third as currency of denomination of international bank loans, with a market share of 2.6%. At the end of 1987, 382 Eurobond issues had been floated for more than 29 billion ECU, and in that year the ECU ranked fifth with a market share of close to 5%.

As of September 30, 1987, all banks reporting to the Bank for International Settlements (BIS) had ECU liabilities for the equivalent of 75.2 billion U.S. dollars and ECU assets for the equivalent of 88.5 billion U.S. dollars, both figures representing new records.

On the Kredietbank's balance sheet, ECU liabilities represent 6% and ECU assets 12% of total footings. We handle a daily average of about 1,350 ECU payments for more than 700 correspondent banks in more than 30 countries, resulting in an average daily turnover of close to 6 billion ECU. At the end of 1987, we had about 6,000 ECU accounts on our books.

The ECU: Stable and European

An appreciation of the ECU, the EMS's linchpin, must start with its definition--that is, the intrinsic features of the ECU defined as a basket of, in principle, all currencies of the EEC, the latter not yet a union but a more or less cohesive group of intensely intertwined economies whose governments have expressed a firm intention to unify eventually. These intrinsic features of the ECU are its built-in stability and its truly European character, as expressed by its composition and the applicable rules of the game. Probably equally important when appreciating the ECU is the official support, not only in word but also in deed, that it gets continuously from the highest European authorities.

The ECU market is continuously expanding and diversifying (deposits, loans, foreign exchange, primary and secondary bond markets, options, futures, credit cards, and traveler's checks), and an ECU clearing system has been put in place, managed by the ECU Banking Association, assisted by SWIFT, and capped by the BIS as agent for about 30 ECU clearing banks, handling about 150,000 ECU payments per month.

It cannot be denied, however, that, so far, use of the ECU has been mainly confined to the financial field and that it has not yet found full expression in commercial transactions (e.g., contracting for goods and services) relating in particular, as would be possible and advisable, to intra-European import and export business. Yet here already there are many inspiring examples of its use.

It must be clear by now that the ECU is on its way to becoming much more than a unit of account for the exclusive use of central banks. More and more economic agents in more and more countries, not just those in the EEC, are using it not only as a unit of account but also as a savings and payment instrument. It is on its way to becoming a true European currency.

Already the ECU is, to a certain degree, Europe's own foreign currency. Eventually, it should also become Europe's own common domestic currency. As its private use expands, the relative importance of all its existing national currencies will diminish. Its components, the national currencies, will fade away. One day, we will reach the point at which the ECU's relative importance will be so big that the creation of a European Federal Reserve System, a truly European Central Bank, will be impossible to postpone any longer.

Such a central bank will have a charter that will guarantee its independence and its professionalism, so that it can issue and control the issue of the real ECU, for which today's basket-type ECU is only a precursor. That real ECU will no longer be defined as a basket but, like any other currency today, as the national currency of the United States of Europe. If it is to be issued and controlled by an independent and professional bank, which will pursue stability in the value of money as its highest priority, the ECU will continue to be a stable, noninflationary unit, not only the domestic currency unit for Europe (i.e., the EEC) but also one of the probably three leading currencies in the world used for international transactions in both the financial and commercial fields.

From Dollar Dominance, via Perestroika, Toward YE$ (Yen-ECU-Dollar)-Troika

As we have seen, the U.S. dollar has lost already quite a bit of its international importance, and rightly so. The Japanese yen has gained already quite a bit in international importance, and also rightly so.

Europe is too important still to remain passive, or even worse, to remain handicapped by its traditional divisions and, as a consequence thereof, unable to participate in the debate to discuss and tackle the world's problems. Its goal of unification, therefore, cannot be a partial one but should eventually be oriented toward a political union. A political union without a monetary union is unthinkable, and monetary union means a European Central Bank and one European currency, most likely the ECU, as the radical expression of its own monetary identity.

Furthering the development of the EMS and the ECU in Europe, while further reducing the importance of the U.S. dollar and raising the importance of the Japanese yen, is going to be a perestroika or reform exercise aimed at reducing an enormous global financial imbalance. Only when the role of the yen, the ECU, and the U.S. dollar can be brought back somewhat more into balance with the underlying economic data can these three currencies together form a troika of more or less equal partners, a YE$-troika that is better equipped for managing a better world.

Notes

[1] Conference on International Banking, Pace University, New York, March 31, 1988.

CHAPTER 5

THE WORLD ECONOMIC AND FINANCIAL SYSTEM: PROGRESS IN INTERNATIONAL COORDINATION AND DEBT FINANCING

Hélène Ploix

Mme. Ploix is the executive director, International Monetary Fund and the World Bank and Affiliates, Washington, DC. Mme. Ploix received a Diplome de l'Institut d'Etudes Politiques in Paris, an MA in Public Administration from the University of California at Berkeley, degrees in law and liberal arts from the Sorbonne, and an MBA from l'Institut European d'Administration des Affaires, Fontainebleau. Among her previous positions are those as management consultant to McKinsey & Company, director of the Compagnie Europeenne de Publication, president and managing director, Banque Industrielle et Mobiliere Privee, and advisor to the Prime Minister for Economic and Financial Affairs of France.

Progress in international coordination and debt financing is at the heart of the activities of the International Monetary Fund (IMF) and the World Bank. I am especially interested in the word "progress," because I was surprised at the time of the September 1987 meeting of the Interim Committee by a journalist's asking me skeptically whether there had actually been any progress at all.

My conviction is that there *has* been progress. In 1985 the first step in international coordination among the five major industrial countries was limited to some interventions on the exchange markets. Today the seven major industrial countries meet regularly to assess current trends and prospects, develop objectives and projections, and review economic policies and performance.

Although progress is more mixed on the debt financing front, it seems to me that during 1986 the debt strategy was a concept empty of content, whereas since 1987, after the Mexican package was settled, the debt strategy has been characterized by innovative techniques. Furthermore, at present the financing gap of the poorest African countries appears to be closing, at least for the short period ahead of us.

This chapter describes in some detail the progress that has been made in the areas of both international coordination and debt financing. This description draws extensively on the work of the IMF, especially the World Economic Outlook, and the work of the World Bank.

Progress in International Coordination

What does progress in international coordination mean, and what are the major steps in this process? What is the role of the IMF? What has been achieved so far, and what remains to be done?

The meaning of policy coordination

In an important paper in 1984, Henry Wallich, a former governor of the U.S. Federal Reserve System, stated: "Coordination, harmonization, cooperation, consultation: these, in descending order, are the terms by which nations...recognize that they are not alone in the world.... Cooperation falls well short of coordination, a concept which implies a significant modification of national policies." I fully subscribe to this definition.

Policy coordination may be viewed as a first step toward a better-functioning and a more up-to-date international monetary order. More specifically, policy coordination means the negotiation and establishment of procedures and arrangements that would allow the major industrial countries to appreciate and be aware of the *international* impact of any policies they take or consider. In other words, countries would move beyond trying to assess only the domestic economic consequences of policy actions. This is obviously very important. As is now generally acknowledged, we live in an increasingly *integrated* world economy. This means that each country is less isolated or protected from actions taken in other countries, in particular if those other countries are economically dominant. Therefore, we need to complement the increasingly close interrelations in the trade and financial links among countries by seeking a way of coordinating those major policy actions that have a direct bearing on trade and finance and, by extension, on other areas of economic activity. Otherwise, international economic relations will become haphazard and unstable and, worse still, even at cross-purposes with policy actions.

Steps in international coordination

The first recent illustration of coordinated actions is the 1978 Bonn economic summit at which Germany agreed on expansionary fiscal actions.

Perhaps the first real developments in the process can be dated to the Plaza Agreement on September 22, 1985, although the announcement circulated at the end of that meeting does not mention coordination. It recalls the commitment to pursue "individually in our own countries and *cooperatively* together, policies conducive to sustained growth and higher employment." It expresses the "view that significant progress has been made" in the ministers' and governors' "efforts to promote a *convergence* of favorable economic performance among their countries."

International policy coordination was the main theme of the Tokyo Economic Summit held in May 1986. The Tokyo summit even designed the procedures for effective coordination:

> It is important that there should be close and continuous coordination of economic policy among the seven summit countries. We welcome the recent examples of improved coordination among the Group of Five Finance Ministers and Central Bankers, which have helped to change the pattern of exchange rates and to lower interest rates on an orderly and non-inflationary basis. We agree, however, that additional measures should be taken to ensure that procedures for effective coordination of international economic policy are strengthened further. To this end, the Heads of State or Government request the seven Finance Ministers to review their individual economic objectives and forecasts collectively at least once a year, using the indicators specified below, with a particular view to examining their mutual compatibility.

The word "coordination" was then explicitly mentioned in the communique issued following the Louvre Accord of February 22, 1987: "The ministers and governors agreed to intensify their economic policy coordination efforts in order to promote more balanced global growth and to reduce existing imbalances." From then on, coordination was mentioned in the first paragraph of all the Group of Seven communiques. For instance, the statement of the Group of Seven of December 22, 1987, often referred to as "Louvre Accord II," restates, "the finance ministers and central bank governors...will continue to carry forward their economic policy coordination efforts in 1988 under the arrangements endorsed at the Venice summit."

The role of the IMF

Policy coordination refers *primarily to a process* among the major industrial countries. An important vehicle for this coordination is the IMF, the institution founded some 45 years ago to be the focus of the international monetary system and to provide a forum for international monetary cooperation. Indeed, the efforts currently under way should be seen as an outgrowth of the Fund's traditional multilateral surveillance work. Like that work, these efforts rest on persuasion rather than coercion or built-in triggering processes. The essence of the Fund's role thus continues to be to analyze, to inform, and to counsel. To what ends? There are three in particular, as follows:

- Identifying inconsistencies in national policies with medium-term objectives for the group as a whole.

- Focusing the attention of each of the major economies on the consequences of its actions not just for the other major economies but also for the rest of the world.

- Reviewing and assessing current trends and helping to determine whether there are significant deviations from an intended course that require consideration of remedial policy action.

In line with all this, the *instruments of coordination* are being developed through the work of the IMF with the concurrence, of course, of the countries involved. Much progress has been made. The more visible example of this is the development of certain economic indicators relating to major economic magnitudes, such as gross national product (GNP), domestic demand, the GNP deflator (which is really a way of measuring inflation), interest rates, exchange rates, and current account balances. Using these indicators in its annual World Economic Outlook exercise (namely, the major annual review and prognosis of the international economic situation undertaken by its staff), the IMF has been able to present a number of "scenarios." These scenarios seek to provide some estimate of how economies will evolve depending on various sets of assumptions.

For example, one scenario projects what will happen to the economies if current policies continue. This is the so-called baseline scenario and perhaps not a very realistic one. Policies do change, and besides, scenarios that indicate large imbalances to be financed are not sustainable, given the likely reaction of financial markets. For that reason, another scenario has been developed to demonstrate what will happen if certain policy actions take place--for example, if the United States takes steps to reduce its budget and trade deficits, or if certain steps are taken in Japan and in the European economies. A third scenario is based on the assumption of financial disruption in the markets. As a result of this exercise, which does not purport to provide an actual forecast, we are able to have at least some idea of the sort of consequences that would flow from different actions (or lack of them) in the major economies.

The results of progress

The results of progress in international coordination are obvious. The material in this section is largely extracted from the work of the IMF staff. The objectives stated for this coordinated effort were to correct the major imbalances in the world economy. Today, it is possible to say that the current stance of policies in the major industrial countries reflect this determination. Fiscal policy has now begun to play a more important role in the adjustment process, with earlier divergences in fiscal stance tending to be reversed. In the United States, the federal budget deficit was reduced by the equivalent of about 2% of GNP in fiscal year 1987. In Japan, fiscal policy in 1987 was oriented toward providing support for the economy. The fiscal situation in the Federal Republic of Germany has changed significantly, too.

Monetary policy is also being actively used as an instrument of policy coordination. Fears of a resurgence of inflationary pressures, as well as a desire to support the U.S. dollar in line with the Louvre Accord, led to a gradual firming of interest rates in the United States during much of 1987. In Japan and Germany, short-term interest-rate differentials widened significantly in favor of dollar-dominated assets.

Furthermore, the analysis of *alternative scenarios* demonstrates that only the implementation of the set of policies consistent with the policy intentions set forth in the Louvre communique in February 1987, and endorsed again by the same countries in their December 22, 1987, statement, will allow for a significant reduction of the external imbalances without adverse effects on other objectives, such as lowering inflation, reducing fiscal deficits, tackling structural rigidities, and sustaining growth. This scenario, based on better-coordinated policies in the industrial countries, will also have beneficial effects for the developing countries in aggregate.

On the other hand, a scenario simulating an upsurge in *protectionism*, when a number of countries raise their tariffs, shows that protectionism is a negative-sum game in which everyone loses. Output would fall more in all countries, and the developing countries would suffer relatively more of a loss in output than would the industrial countries as a group.

Finally, as regards the developing world, the environment created by coordinated policies in industrial countries, complemented by the continuation of adjustment efforts in developing countries and combined with some recovery in their terms of trade, led in 1987 to the first significant fall in debt-export ratios since 1980. This reduction in the debt ratio is projected to continue in 1988 and 1989.

What remains to be done?

The French Minister of Finance, Mr. Balladur, expressed his views in The Wall Street Journal of February 23, 1988, on the desirable next step in international coordination. Because "the Western world has been weakened over the past 15 years by the monetary and economic disorders caused by the refusal to accept a common discipline," he proposed to rebuild an international monetary system. Because the ultimate effectiveness of the present system rests on the willingness of the participating countries, he suggested that governments work together toward a true international monetary system that would entail automatic mechanisms and sanctions. It could draw on the experience of the European Monetary System or be organized around a standard that would play the role of main world reserve asset.

Progress in Debt Financing

The year 1987 was a pivotal one, but additional steps are required to increase the desired momentum.

Debt financing is only one aspect of the debt strategy. I have just commented indirectly on another aspect by indicating how increased coordination of policies was conducive to a more favorable external economic environment. Adjustment in debtor countries is another essential feature. There is not space to tackle that subject here, but it is clear that it is at the root of any progress in the overall debt strategy.

Debt financing is very different when considering the low-income countries or the highly indebted middle-income countries. The first group, the low-income countries, is indebted essentially to public creditors and receives long-term multilateral assistance at very concessional rates. These countries are located mainly in sub-Saharan Africa, but Pakistan, Bangladesh, Sri Lanka, and Bolivia, for instance, also belong to this group where income per capita is less than $835.

The strategy of James A. Baker, III, Secretary of the U.S. Treasury, concerns the highly indebted middle-income countries. These countries are Latin America, with the exception of Nigeria, Cote d' Ivoire, Yugoslavia, and Morocco. Most of their debt is owed to commercial banks at market rates. They borrow from the World Bank and other development banks at close to market rates.

Although mixed, progress in debt financing can be seen in both groups.

Debt financing in low-income countries

In 1986 and 1987, significant steps were taken to alleviate the situation in low-income countries and to hold out reasonable promise that far-reaching policy reforms will be supported by creditors in a timely and appropriate manner. Five developments represent important progress in dealing with the debt of low-income countries, as follows:

1. The International Development Association, the concessional window of the World Bank Group, was replenished by $12.4 billion, 50% of which would be allocated to sub-Saharan Africa. This eighth replenishment became operational in September 1987 and will be disbursed over a three-year period.

2. At the end of 1987, with the establishment of the enhanced structural adjustment facility of the Fund, the resources that had been available under the structural adjustment facility were more than tripled. The additional $8.4 billion secured will allow the Fund to support macroeconomic and structural reforms in low-income countries at concessional rates, thereby facilitating these countries' growth out of their debt.

3. In late December 1987, the World Bank succeeded in securing commitments of $6.4 billion from bilateral donors, the European Community, and the African Development Bank to address the financing needs of the debt-distressed low-income countries of sub-Saharan Africa. This financial assistance will be concessional, quick disbursing, and will cofinance adjustment operations of the World Bank. This will lead to about $3 billion additional external resources to these countries over the three-year period 1988 to 1990. Two features of this program must be outlined: first, for the first time, most

of the bilateral donors will finance adjustment programs, whereas their lending has been limited to project financing previously; second, this assistance will be in the form of grants or concessional loans, whereas in the past some bilateral donors have not subsidized their loans to that extent.

4. Official creditors have, on a case-by-case basis, agreed to extend the maturity and the grace periods up to 20 years and 10 years, respectively, when rescheduling the debt of low-income countries that are undertaking adjustment programs. They have also agreed to reschedule official development assistance at concessional rates and to convert some loans into grants.

5. Other helpful developments have included the provision of financial resources by donor countries to allow Bolivia to buy back its own debt.

Debt financing in middle-income countries

Progress has been mixed in middle-income countries. The Bretton Woods institutions are active supporters of and participants in the debt strategy elaborated by Secretary Baker of the United States in Seoul in September 1985. It is based on a case-by-case approach to countries with debt problems. It involves the carrying out of programs of economic adjustment by debtor countries, the provisioning of financing by commercial banks, and the support (both financial and policy advice) of the IMF and the World Bank. The principal objective of this approach has been to encourage a return to normal creditor-debtor relationships--that is, a situation where developing countries will attract the financing that they need for their development in amounts that will not cause recurrent payment difficulties. A fundamental premise of this approach is that strong and sustained adjustment will always be backed by adequate financial support.

If two recent developments could raise some doubts on the chances to carry out this strategy smoothly, progress is shown in other areas and gives hope to see the light at the end of the tunnel.

Lately, financing packages have become more difficult to arrange and interest arrears have emerged; interest arrears have been used by some debtor countries as a source of financing. In addition, some banks have increased their loss-loan provisions beyond regulatory requirements; others have sold their portfolio at a loss. These banks have shown thereby some doubts about the capacity of the concerned indebted countries to repay their debt. However, by the same token, they have strengthened their balance sheet and might become more active in using different market-based instruments. This is the positive side of the coin. In parallel, we have observed a greater diversification of the debt approach, which has evolved in many ways in order to satisfy financial institutions' constraints and objectives in a flexible way while providing the indebted countries with the necessary additional financing. To be effective, these new options, often termed the "menu approach," have to be market-based and entered into voluntarily by a debtor and its creditors. This approach has allowed the debtor country either directly or indirectly to benefit in part from existing discounts, because a secondary market has emerged for bank claims of developing countries that have experienced debt servicing difficulties. Such options include debt conversion schemes, buy-backs, securitization, and exit bonds. The Mexican deal arranged by Morgan Guaranty Trust in late December 1987, whereby Mexico exchanged some of its debt for bonds, the payment of principal on which is backed by U.S. Treasury securities, is the latest and most innovative example (as of Spring 1988).

Chile best illustrates the impact of these options within the framework of the overall debt strategy. Because Chile has implemented the appropriate macroeconomic policies, it has been able to reduce its old debt by $3 billion and to reduce its overall stock of debt to commercial banks from $12.6 billion in 1986 to $10.6 billion today.

One should not underestimate the banking community's ability to fashion new instruments and approaches, particularly with the continued help of their supervisory authorities.

As concerns "adaptations" by the Fund, a number of efforts are under way to strengthen the ability and willingness of the indebted countries to implement sound macroeconomic policies and needed structural reforms, and thereby to give a new impetus to the debt strategy. In particular, the Fund is currently considering ways of revamping its longer-term extended facility and is also seeking ways to ensure that adjustment programs in effect are not derailed by external developments over which debtor countries have no control. It is also examining the instruments it uses for monitoring programs--including, in particular, its well-known performance tests, or conditionality--with a view to ensuring that they do not deter countries from approaching the Fund and putting programs in place in a timely manner. The World Bank, for its part, has also been increasing its assistance in the area of structural and sectoral adjustment. Over the period 1985-1987, the World Bank and the other multilateral development banks have increased their share of net flows to 50% of total medium- and long-term flows, compared with roughly 12% in 1980-1982. Net financing of the World Bank can be expected to be about $3 billion annually over the next five years, thanks to the proposed general capital increase that has just been secured. If the increase is approved by parliaments, the World Bank capital will be increased by $74.8 billion to reach $171.4 billion.

Although debt problems have not been definitely resolved, it must be recognized that here too a great deal of progress has been made, and, inevitably, this has not been cost-free. Many countries have undertaken courageous adjustment policies, and there is now a greater realism about the need to reorient policies. And, external adjustment *is* taking place. Consider the large, heavily indebted middle-income countries. Since the onset of the debt crisis, they have absorbed a cumulative deterioration in their terms of trade of more than 20%, or the equivalent of 3% of gross domestic product (GDP), and they have still recorded a strengthening in their combined current account of close to 5% of GDP. This is a considerable achievement and one that is too often overlooked.

This is why a second approach, which has been much talked about, is not acceptable, especially to creditor governments. It would involve the establishment of comprehensive solutions, generally in some form of debt financing facility that would take up the debt of the developing countries. The Bretton Woods institutions and creditor governments have, in general, been opposed to such an approach in that it would apply the same solution to all countries irrespective of their economic situation and prospects, or needs, and hence would provide a disincentive for those countries that are able to service their debt. A third factor against this approach has been that it would require, directly or indirectly, the expenditure of public funds at a time when many budgets are under pressure.

We can conclude by recognizing that we are not out of the woods. Progress has been uneven, and in many cases the economic situation remains vulnerable--especially to potential developments such as an increase in protectionism. But we *are* making progress. We *are* moving toward policy coordination among the rich countries, finding more flexible solutions for the middle-income countries, and providing greater financing for the low-income countries. We must foster and support these efforts and not allow ourselves to be defeated by pessimism.

PART II

FOREIGN EXCHANGE MARKETS

CHAPTER 6

THE GROWTH AND CHANGING CHARACTER OF THE FOREIGN EXCHANGE MARKET

Sam Y. Cross

Mr. Cross is an executive vice-president of the Federal Reserve Bank of New York and senior officer in charge of the bank's foreign operations. He is responsible for relations with other central banks, the maintenance of foreign official and international accounts with the New York Federal Reserve, and the foreign exchange operations of the Federal Reserve, including those of the U.S. Treasury. Mr. Cross joined the bank after seven years as an executive director of the International Monetary Fund. Before that, Mr. Cross was a career official of the U.S. Treasury Department.

One reason why it is a pleasure to contribute to this book on international banking and capital markets is that there is so much happening in financial markets these days, so much to discuss and debate. And the changes are taking place so rapidly. Indeed, in some of these markets nowadays, when you hear the old-timers reminisce nostalgically about the old days, you may find that some of the old-timers are only about 29 years of age. And those simpler, more tranquil days of the past were only five or ten years ago!

Certainly we have been living through a period of revolution in the financial field, a revolution that has altered our financial system in many ways. This chapter comments first on the extensiveness of the changes that are now taking place. Then it discusses some of the implications for financial markets and the global economy, as well as some of the concerns and responsibilities of the authorities with respect to the financial and payments system.

We focus first on the foreign exchange market and describe some of the ways in which that particular market has been transformed in the past decade. Some of the changes that have taken place in the past 10 years are discussed.

1. There has been an enormous change in the sheer size of the foreign exchange market. For the U.S. market, the Federal Reserve Bank of New York (FRBNY) makes a survey every three years. Our most recent survey is now two years old, so we are not up to date, but we estimate that turnover has grown by ten- to twelvefold in the past decade. At the same time, we have seen a much greater dispersion of the U.S. market, spreading outside of New York into other parts of the country. We have also seen the entry of many new institutions into the trading community, not only a lot more banks but also new groups such as the investment banks have increased their role. As far as the present size of the worldwide market is concerned, we can only guess, but I hear estimates of turnover at levels up to $400 billion a day--again, multiples of the level a decade ago.

2. There has been a considerable rearrangement in the currency focus on the market, largely as a result of the following factors:

- A gradual relative decline in the continental currencies as trading in that group has tended to become more concentrated in the mark.
- The greater role of the yen and its emergence as the second most widely traded nondollar currency.
- The emergence and expansion into capital markets of a number of so-called exotic currencies, in particular the Australian dollar, the Scandinavian currencies, and the Spanish peseta.

3. A third development is that the 24-hour market has become an operational reality. The very rapid growth of the Asian markets and the emergence of new trading centers in the Australia/New Zealand time zone now bridge the gap in business hours between New York's closing and Tokyo's opening, giving us a seamless flow of activity.

4. There is now a much greater diversity in the instruments used in foreign exchange trading, particularly the growth in futures and options, with all the complexities those instruments entail in terms of law, accounting, and operating technique. For example, when banks first became involved with options, they tended to be writers of options--that is, they offered options to their customers who bought options seeking to hedge exposures. More recently, many banks have themselves become buyers of options, using the instrument as a means of positioning in volatility. Futures have also become much more widely used by market professionals to hedge exposure. The result is a marked improvement in the liquidity of the futures market and a closer integration of the futures market with the traditional spot foreign exchange market. In recent years, the futures market seems to have become a less segregated market, with less likelihood that it can go off in directions on its own.

5. There has been an important change in the customer base in the foreign exchange market. There is no longer such heavy reliance on corporate importers and exporters. A major role is now played by

the portfolio investors, the life insurance companies, the investment houses, and the pension funds, as securitization has developed and investment flows have mushroomed. This has major implications for the market.

6. In the field of information, access has broadened considerably, and sophisticated mechanisms for organization and management of the information have been developed. With the wider use of video, a vast amount of information--and *mis*information--from all over the world is instantaneously available to more and more market participants. And there is a greater need to organize and manage these data, to cope with what can become an information overload. This need has fostered the development of digital technology, permitting direct input of information into computers, and the development of software to filter the information, record it, prioritize it, and manipulate it. These developments have facilitated the growth of charting and technical analysis, which have grown in use and popularity as the belief in mechanical explanations of exchange rate behavior has gained favor.

I could go on and cite the moves toward contract netting as concerns over payments disruptions and credit limits problems have multiplied, the introduction of taping to help deal with disputed transactions, and so on. The evidence all points to the same conclusion--that we have seen in the past 10 years a major transformation in the foreign exchange market: its structure, its size, its character, its complexity, and its sophistication.

What I have described with respect to changes occurring in the foreign exchange market is true of other international financial markets across the board. All the financial markets are being transformed. I need not enumerate here all the factors that have brought about these changes because that story is well known and amply documented. During the past decade, the environment has been ideal for innovation, and the result has been a period of great creativity and ferment. With respect to the causal factors, I will not list them, but I will emphasize one point: that it was the interaction and interplay of these factors, working together and feeding off each other in a dynamic way, that brought about the changed environment. Thus, we had a world of very large international payments imbalances, which provided fertile ground for the invention of new financial products and instruments. Among other things, this helped to encourage the move toward deregulation, which led to additional new products. That permitted the financing of still larger imbalances. Added to this are the longer-term trends toward improved technology that have lowered transactions costs--in some cases to a tenth or a fiftieth of the levels of two decades ago. In addition, there has been the growing worldwide institutionalization of savings and the diversification of investment. All these and a variety of other factors have played off each other in a way that has transformed the entire financial landscape of which the foreign exchange market is one integral part.

It was particularly in the early part of the 1980s that the range of financial products widened so greatly. In those years, the "rocket" scientists (financial innovators specializing in techniques) engaged in an enormous amount of "unbundling" and "rebundling." That is to say, they were separating the credit mechanism into its individual elements and regrouping various components into imaginative and attractive packages. By this means, they were able to splice together different combinations of warrants, options, swaps, and indexes, and to fashion products to meet the needs of almost any investor or borrower, whatever the expectations about interest rates, exchange rates, asset prices, or tax or regulatory obstacles the investor faced. More recently the pace of change has become less feverish, with some financial markets experiencing a period of consolidation or shakeout. Activity is much lower in some areas, and some of the new products have failed to thrive in the changing economic climate.

Even so, there continue to be rapid strides toward global integration of financial markets. Although the speed of change differs considerably from one country to another, almost all are affected. It is hard to see how any major industrial country could fully resist, even if it wanted to. New financial instruments, often developed in major centers such as New York or London, quickly find application in markets throughout the world. And large international companies, wherever headquartered, demand the full range of services, with the result that competition among suppliers of financial services tends to bring a quick geographical spreading of any new innovations. The cumulative result is that in virtually all major industrial countries there are the same trends toward deregulation, toward innovation, toward global market integration. In the United States, Britain, France, Germany, Italy, and Japan, there are the same unmistakable trends even though the stage of development and the pace of change vary greatly from country to country.

The large volume of transactions in what have become globally integrated financial markets has important implications for the payments and settlements machinery, particularly the large dollar payments system that underlies that machinery. In New York, we are particularly sensitive to those implications because we now have in the Federal Reserve Bank's electronic payments system and in the New York Clearing House CHIPS system payments that easily total \$1.5 trillion a day--a figure that works out to around \$300 every business day for every man, woman, and child on Earth. That figure of \$1.5 trillion a day has increased by about 5,000% since 1970. These large dollar payments systems bring together all major financial institutions--the banks and securities houses--on a worldwide basis. Interlocking exposures link financial centers, and 24-hour trading puts New York at the end of the clock and, in settlements, at the end of the line. These payments systems, given their speed, size, and interdependence, are obviously sensitive to a major liquidity problem of a direct participant, and even temporary mechanical failures in a computer can be disruptive beyond the institution where the original breakdown occurs.

What are we--the central bankers and officials--doing and what should we be doing to respond to the changed conditions that we now face in the financial markets? What should be our attitude toward the changes that are taking place? The central banks should not try to halt innovation and change, even if they have the ability and the authority to do so. We all know there are great benefits in having our adaptable and resilient financial system. And no one would fail to recognize that the changes we have seen in recent years have brought to the individual users of financial services the benefits of broader, deeper, more liquid markets, a wider and more flexible range of hedging, and trading opportunities, cost savings, and efficiency.

There are, however, nagging and unanswered questions of whether these changes do not also bring certain risks and vulnerabilities--not only for an individual firm, but more important, in the aggregate effects for the financial system as a whole. Central bankers are by nature worriers, and we have to be concerned about the size and volatility of these markets, the diversity of instruments, and the management of various kinds of risk. Redistributing risk does not mean eliminating it. There are new instruments and techniques that have not been tested over time under differing economic conditions. And the legal and accounting treatment of these instruments and techniques is not always certain. It is by no means certain that each and every new product of financial engineering, despite its efficiency, necessarily improves our financial system. Someone has said that attaching jet engines to a tricycle will give a faster means of travel, but it hardly gives you a better transportation system!

Of course, that's a foolish analogy. At some point, however, you do have to ask yourself: What does all this mean? Is the global village better off if FOREX turnover is $300 billion per day rather than $200 billion, or if a transaction is arranged at 10 pips instead of 20? Beyond a certain point, is all the financial wizardry really producing net benefits outside the financial community? Perhaps we have become mesmerized by the elegance of new financial products and are missing the larger concerns of producing goods and services more efficiently, spreading consumption possibilities more widely, and investing in the future more usefully. More bluntly, does shaving a few more basis points off borrowing costs through a swap help to produce better cars or more houses? Certainly the world needs efficient money and capital markets but not at the expense of diverting too much attention, talent, and resources from other pressing problems. I sometimes wonder if we are not in danger of doing so.

On balance, innovation is certainly beneficial--up to a point--and inevitable. Our challenge is to channel these creative forces into beneficial uses so that they not only improve the efficiency and profitability of the financial system but do so in a way that maintains the system's strength and stability as well. For those persons on the central banking side, that requires actions on various fronts, e.g., in bank supervision, in our activities with respect to the payments system, and in policy coordination with other central banks. And we are moving on those fronts and others to try to deal better with today's problems and realities.

One area in which there is the promise of real progress is in bank supervision. The recent effort by the authorities of the Group of Ten to move toward convergence and to adopt comparable risk-based capital adequacy standards for internationally active banks is an important breakthrough. Given the differing types of banking systems in the G-10 countries and the complexity of the subject, the problems should not be underrated. If it can be achieved, success can move us toward a more rational worldwide system. It would put virtually all the world's major banking institutions on a similar foundation for measuring capital adequacy. Also, because it applies to both balance sheet and off-balance sheet activities, it adapts supervisory standards to new activities and new instruments that have developed in recent years.

A second area where progress is being made is in the operation of the payments system, to deal better with overdrafts, management of credit risk, and operational requirements. A third area in which the central banks can play a key role is in the strengthening of policy coordination and implementation internationally. This is a subject that brings sighs of skepticism from many audiences. And understandably so, for the task of coordination is a formidable one. Yet through the various groups of countries real progress is possible.

Over the years, understanding among the major nations of one another's problems, prospects, and points of view has improved, and we have become more open in dealing with these matters. In daily operations (certainly in foreign exchange, the area with which I am most familiar), discussions and contacts are frequent and extensive. My colleagues at FRBNY regularly start telephoning their counterparts at other central banks at 5:00 or 6:00 A.M., calling either from their homes or from our trading room to get an assessment of conditions in those markets. And they follow up with conversations throughout the day. When the markets are active, those calls can continue throughout the night. These links are of value to all of us in helping us to understand these markets and coordinate our operations.

Let us turn to a different and broader aspect of the subject and ask this question: If we postulate continued strides toward globally integrated and deregulated capital markets, a world of larger and larger capital flows, where are these changes likely to lead us? What are the implications for how our economies are managed and how the financial system operates? A full treatment of this subject is not appropriate or possible in this book, but we can discuss two points.

A first question is: What are the implications for international adjustment, for the way nations adjust their economies to external disequilibria? One point is quite obvious. Clearly, the markets of today, large and efficient as they are, can and do provide much more capability for the private financing of imbalances--at least when the sun is shining and the winds are fair and the markets are willing to provide that financing. There is more "play" in the system, and nations are able to finance much larger disequilibria with private capital flows than they could before. Current account surpluses and deficits that can be financed by private markets and private capital flows are at levels many times higher than those of 10 years ago. There is another side to this matter, however. We know also that market conditions can change suddenly and that market perceptions of creditworthiness can shift abruptly. Many Latin American borrowers learned that in 1982. The financial markets, which have become so large and efficient, can provide more freedom but they can also take it away. Depending on the market's assessment of a borrower's policies and prospects, it can at times postpone the need for adjustment by making funding available and at other times hasten or compel adjustment by withdrawing that financing.

A second question is: What are the effects on the conduct of monetary policy of the move toward massive and globally integrated capital markets? It seems that in some countries money becomes harder to measure, and traditional relationships (e.g., between money and spending) are shifted or upset by the innovations and structural adjustments in our financial markets. In addition, it appears that in some countries the relative importance of the exchange rate as a channel through which monetary and financial policy has its effect on the economy has risen along with the increase in international capital mobility. For some of the smaller, more open economies, developments in the external sector have always played this more important role. For other countries, the change may be more noticeable. In a sense, with global financial integration, each nation may be becoming more of a "small country" and more subject to the external influences of what has become a very large international market. This lessening of national autonomy only means that we are becoming a more interdependent world--a move that can yield great advantages. But it does emphasize the necessity of our understanding and taking the necessary steps to cope with that greater dependence.

In thinking about the growing significance of capital flows in our world of globally integrated capital markets, it is worth standing back to reflect on how dramatically conditions and our attitudes have changed over the past several decades. Forty years ago when the International Monetary Fund (IMF) was created, when the present world monetary order was originally constructed, the emphasis was overwhelmingly on international trade in goods and services. The prevailing philosophy focused on freeing merchandise trade and the current account. That was the paramount objective. On the basis of memories of the 1930s, capital transfers were viewed with skepticism and suspicion. In the early days of the IMF, controls on capital flows were tolerated or even encouraged as a means of keeping trade moving and the current account free of restrictions. Today, that thinking has been turned completely around. There is now such freedom for international capital flows, and such massive capital flows, that in a sense they can drive and determine the current account. We see month after month successive moves by one nation after another to liberalize capital markets and capital flows. We also hear, however, calls for protection against the related trade imbalances. The drive toward liberalized global capital markets will certainly move us toward a more integrated and market-determined world economy.

Trade protectionism can move us in quite the opposite direction, however, and that we must guard against.

As we look ahead, the future as always is murky. One of my more visionary colleagues contends that the time will come when we view the world not as nation states trading goods and services with each other but as a complex multinational banking system in which goods and services move from one place to another to offset residual financial imbalances! I certainly do not share that view, and I do not believe he is serious, but clearly the relative significance of capital flows is increasing greatly. The question is whether that shift will occur in a way that will lead toward the more interdependent world that has long been an objective, leading toward that goal by the path of deregulation and opening of markets, rather than by imposing exchange rate rules or other rules that are favored by so many schemes and grand designs for reform.

CHAPTER 7

THE FALL OF THE DOLLAR AND HIGH U.S. INTEREST RATES: TWO INTERPRETATIONS

Ronald I. McKinnon

Dr. McKinnon is professor of economics at Stanford University. He received an engineering diploma from Royal Roads, Victoria, British Columbia, a BA in economics from the University of Alberta, and a PhD in economics from the University of Minnesota. He has contributed extensively to the top academic journals in the areas of international trade and finance, monetary theory and policy, capital markets in less developed countries, and the world financial system. Dr. McKinnon has served as a consultant to U.S. Aid in Korea, the Stanford Research Institute, the World Bank in Ethiopia, the governments of Colombia, Kuwait, Chile, Uraguay, Peru, and the OAS, the International Monetary Fund, and the World Bank in Korea.

More puzzling than the mid-October 1987 crash in the American stock market were the financial events that preceded it. Throughout 1987 to the beginning of October, interest rates on dollar assets rose sharply--particularly on long-term bonds and mortgages. Beginning at less than 8% in early January 1987, interest yields on 30-year U.S. Treasury bonds peaked at about 10.4% two days before the crash on October 19. But stock prices had seemed oblivious and had kept bubbling upward. Stock yields, measured by earnings as a proportion of current prices, fell below 5% by late August--far below returns on bonds.

When the huge "correction" occurred, not only did stock prices plummet (thus raising yields on stocks), but the prices of relatively safe long-term bonds rose sharply. Within a few days in October, interest rates on long-term U.S. Treasury bonds had fallen as low as 8.8%--a fall of 11/2 points within an unprecedented short period. Whether interpreted as a flight to safety or to higher yields, a sharp shift in portfolio preferences from stocks to bonds dramatically narrowed the yield gap between them.

What, then, are the implications for a cyclical downturn in the American (and world) economy--possibly led by further declines in the American stock market? Clearly, if U.S. long-term interest rates stay high or begin increasing, an investment slump and continued financial crisis seem likely.

In early 1988, the Reagan administration took the unprecedented step of openly criticizing the U.S. Federal Reserve System for keeping interest rates too high in 1987. On February 19, the economic report of the president from the Council of Economic Advisers (CEA) was introduced by a letter signed by the president saying: "The prospects for growth in the immediate future have been diminished somewhat by last year's plunge in the stock market, as well as by the increase in interest rates and tightening of monetary policy during 1987."[1] The body of the report explicitly criticized the Fed for letting growth in the monetary aggregates slow too much in 1987, and thus, so it claims, forcing up U.S. interest rates unduly.

Is the CEA's criticism of the Fed correct? What view the Fed takes is critical for determining U.S. monetary policy in 1988, but what happened in 1987 can be interpreted differently. I argue that the Reagan administration's own policy toward the dollar exchange rate, and not the Fed, was responsible for unnecessarily high U.S. interest rates.

Interest Rates and Exchange Rate Expectations

As in Europe and Japan, American interest rates are now sensitive to how the financial markets perceive that the dollar exchange rate will move through time. Bonds denominated in marks, yen, or sterling are close substitutes in international asset portfolios. Furthermore, everybody understands that American monetary policy, in conjunction with those of Germany (representing the EMS bloc) and Japan, has a first-order impact on the dollar exchange rate against marks, sterling, or yen. Therefore, the American government's perception of what is a proper intermediate- or long-term foreign exchange "equilibrium" is a critical determinant of both the term structure of U.S. interest rates and the spot exchange rate. In particular, whether private exchange rate expectations are *regressive* or *extrapolative* determines whether U.S. interest rates fall or rise in response to, say, a depreciation of the dollar.

To illustrate this important point, consider the behavior of U.S. long-term interest rates during the great fall of the dollar that began in March 1985 (Figures 7-1, 7-2, and 7-3). Initially, everybody perceived that, at 260 yen and 3.3 marks, the dollar was grossly overvalued by any unambiguous commodity market criterion--such as purchasing power parity. Anticipating future devaluation, U.S. long-term interest rates were 4% to 5% higher than German or Japanese rates.

Figure 7-1a: LONG-TERM INTEREST RATES IN GERMANY, JAPAN, AND THE UNITED STATES

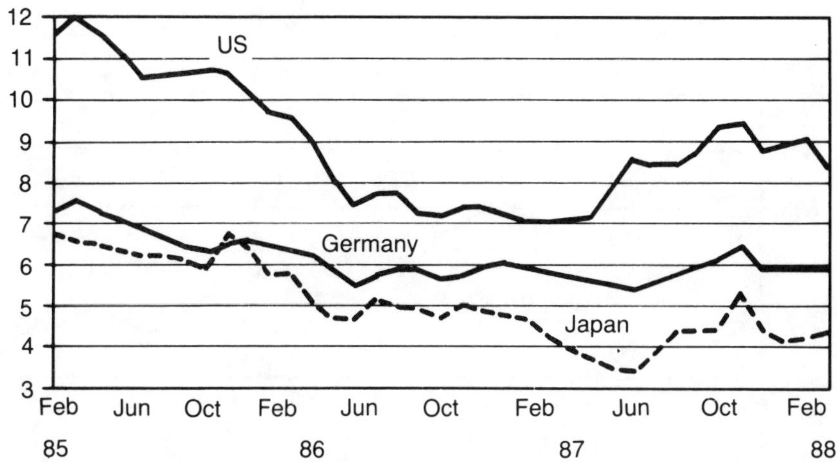

Figure 7-1b: SHORT-TERM INTEREST RATES IN GERMANY, JAPAN, AND THE UNITED STATES

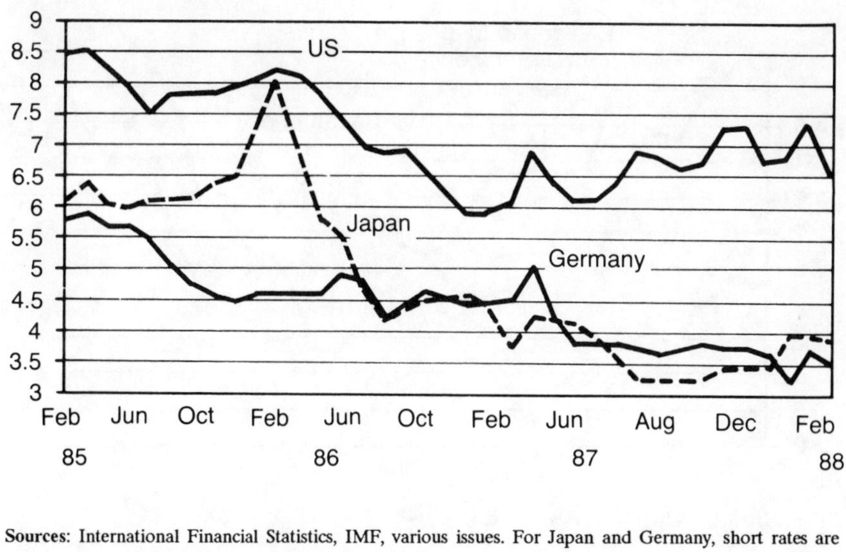

Sources: International Financial Statistics, IMF, various issues. For Japan and Germany, short rates are money market rates; for the United States, short rates are federal funds rates. Long rates are long-term government bond yields. Data since December 1987 are from *The Economist.*

Figure 7-2a: SPOT YEN/$ RATE 80

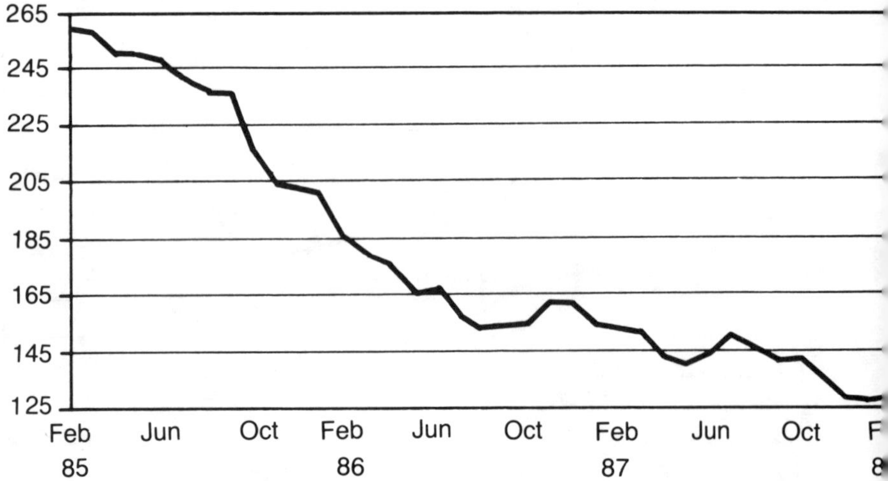

Figure 7-2b: UNITED STATES-JAPAN SHORT-TERM AND LONG-TERM INTEREST DIFFERENTIALS

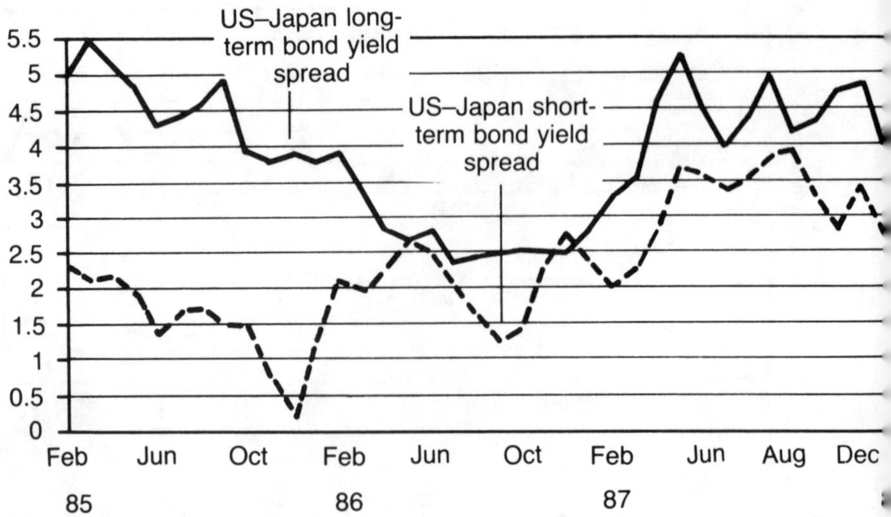

Figure 7-3a: SPOT DM/$ RATE 80

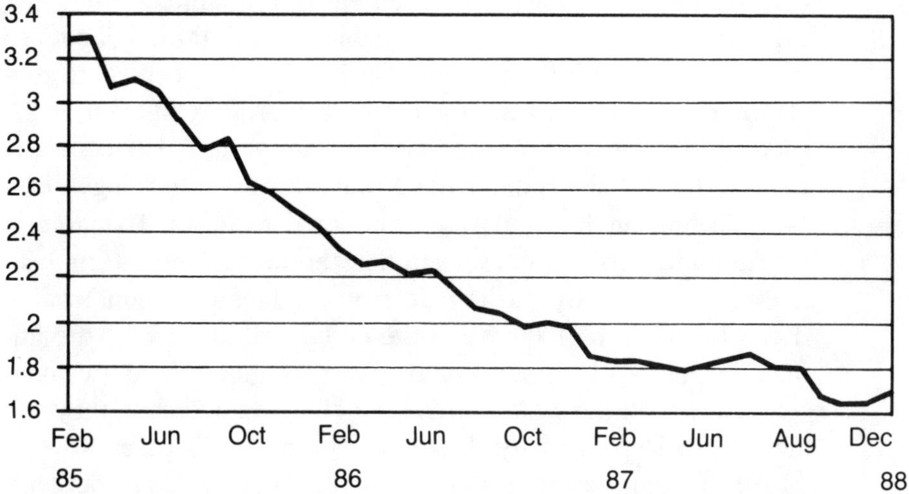

Figure 7-3b: UNITED STATES-GERMAN SHORT-TERM AND LONG-TERM INTEREST DIFFERENTIALS

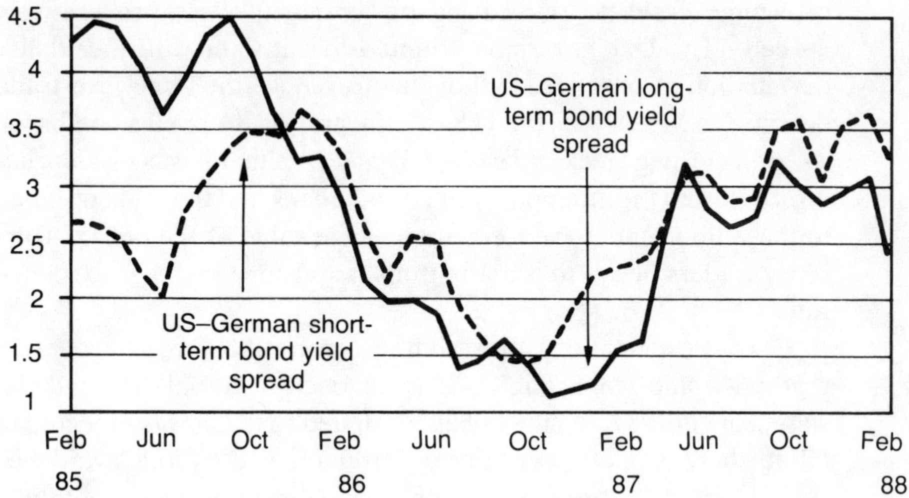

When central banks began cooperating in 1985 to drive the dollar down (as subsequently ratified by the Plaza Hotel Accord the following September), with high money growth in the United States and relative tightness in Germany and Japan, people initially believed there existed an implicit (or secret explicit) official agreement to support some rough target zone for the dollar--around 200 yen or 2.3 marks--which approximated purchasing power parity.[2] Hence, as the dollar fell, the probability of further devaluations over the longer term initially declined in the minds of international investors. To maintain balance in international asset portfolios, therefore, longer-term U.S. interest rates fell relative to their German and Japanese counterparts.

Even for much of 1986, when the dollar had fallen past the imagined target level, international investors maintained (weakly) regressive expectations. Although the dollar had overshot, they saw some substantial probability of its increasing again. Thus, by November 1986, U.S. interest rates had fallen to between 1 and 11/2 percentage points above their mark and yen equivalents.

Beginning in early 1987 with the dollar down to about 150 yen and 2.0 marks, however, these regressive (and stabilizing) expectations of returning closer to purchasing power parity were progressively eroded. The U.S. government hinted that it wanted further dollar devaluation in order (so it thought) to reduce the American trade deficit. On January 13, the U.S. administration dropped a bombshell with a front-page leak in *The New York Times* that it was disassociating itself from the attempts by the Bundesbank and the Bank of Japan to put a floor under the foreign exchange value of the dollar. Currency traders began to see a bottomless pit for the dollar exchange rate.

Private expectations then shifted (on net balance) from being regressive and stabilizing in 1986 to being extrapolative and destabilizing in 1987. As the dollar continued to fall, it was expected to fall further. The effects of this unfortunate, and entirely avoidable, shift in private expectations in the financial markets were twofold.

First, the natural flow of foreign private finance to cover the huge current account deficit in U.S. international payments dried up in 1987. Although difficult to measure precisely, enormous official intervention of over $70 billion--mainly through a rapid buildup of dollar exchange reserves by Japan and European countries--more than covered the U.S. trade deficit until the end of May (Table 7-1).

Table 7-1: FOREIGN EXCHANGE RESERVES HELD OUTSIDE THE UNITED STATES, 1980-1987 (billion dollars, end-period)

	1980	1982	1984	1985	1986	May 1987	Dec. 86- May 87 Change	1987	Dec. 86- Dec. 87 Change
Japan	24.6	23.3	26.4	26.7	42.3	68.8	26.5	81.0	38.7
Taiwan	0.2	0.5	15.7	22.6	46.3	59.9	13.6	70.1[a]	23.8
Germany	48.6	44.8	40.1	44.4	51.7	63.4	11.6	79.3	27.6
UK	20.7	12.4	9.4	12.9	18.4	29.1	10.7	41.7	23.3
Italy	23.1	14.1	20.8	15.5	20.0	24.1	4.1	30.2	12.2
S. Arabia	23.4	29.5	24.7	25.0	18.3	20.5	2.2	22.7	4.4
Netherlands	11.6	10.1	9.2	10.8	11.2	13.2	2.0	16.0	4.8
Sweden	3.4	3.5	3.8	5.8	6.6	8.4	1.8	8.2	1.6
Canada	3.0	3.0	2.5	2.5	3.3	4.9	1.6	7.3	4.0
Belgium	7.8	3.9	4.6	4.8	5.5	6.8	1.3	9.6	4.1
Australia	1.7	6.4	7.4	5.8	7.2	8.3	1.1	8.7	1.5
Spain	11.9	7.7	12.0	11.2	14.8	18.3	3.9	28.2	13.4
France	27.3	16.5	20.9	26.6	31.5	31.5	0.1	29.8[b]	-1.7
S. Korea	2.9	2.8	2.8	2.9	3.3	3.4	0.0	3.6	0.3
Venezuela	6.6	6.6	8.9	10.3	6.4	5.7	-0.7	6.0	-0.4
Brazil	5.8	3.9	11.5	10.6	5.8	4.7	-1.1	6.1[c]	0.3
Switzerland	15.7	15.5	15.3	18.0	21.8	19.8	-2.0	27.5	5.7
Total	238.5	204.5	236.1	256.2	314.3	390.3	76.4	476.0	161.7
Total, excl. Taiwan	238.2	204.0	220.5	233.7	268.0	330.8	62.8	405.9	137.9

Source: International Financial Statistics and Central Bank of China Financial Statistics. Updated from Stephen Marris, *Dollars and Deficits*, Aug. 1987.

Note: Covers only major holders of foreign exchange reserves, ranked by change from Dec. 1986-May 1987.
[a] October 1987.
[b] November 1987.
[c] August 1987.

Second, from late March to mid-May, U.S. long-term interest rates ratcheted upward--while long rates on yen and mark bonds actually fell! By the end of May, the spread in the long-term Eurobond markets had widened again between 4 and 41/2 percentage points, with even wider spreads between certain classes of foreign and domestic government securities.

Perhaps because of an increase in the price of oil and other primary commodities, the dollar strengthened a bit in June and July 1987. Because Japan's and Germany's trade surpluses were suddenly reduced, yen and mark assets became less attractive to international investors. This enabled foreign central banks to unwind some of their previous rapid accumulation of dollar exchange reserves. Long-term interest rates on dollar assets fell modestly, with an increase in Japanese interest rates, as anticipated appreciation in the yen lessened somewhat.

From August through October, however, the dollar weakened again as U.S. officials--and many professional economists such as Martin Feldstein, former chairman of the U.S. Council of Economic Advisers--once more advocated further dollar devaluation to correct the trade deficit. United States interest then rose sharply again, eventually pricking the bubble in the stock market. However, the actual day of the crash on October 19 seemed to have been precipitated, in part, by Secretary James Baker's threatening--over the weekend of October 17 to 18--to cancel the already shaky Louvre Accord (of the preceding February) to put some kind of floor under the dollar. No wonder international investors in dollar assets became nervous!

After the crash, the dollar fell to new lows of around 123 yen and 1.58 marks in late December. Indeed, spokesmen for the U.S. Federal Reserve System said explicitly that the Fed would no longer try to defend the dollar in the foreign exchanges but would concentrate on pumping liquidity into the American financial system to offset the contractionary effects of the crash in the stock market. Unsurprisingly, in late November through December 1987, U.S. long-term interest rates resumed edging upward.

In summary, exchange rate expectations became unnecessarily volatile (extrapolative) in 1987 and seriously undermined the stability of financial markets in the United States, Japan, and Europe: what I call the "falling dollar" interpretation of high U.S. interest rates. Such adverse expectations were (are) provoked by the fear that the American government had adopted the trade balance theory of the "equilibrium" dollar exchange rate--which, if wrong, could lead to indefinite dollar devaluation. Consequently, the natural inflow of private foreign finance, which had more or less covered the American current account deficit from 1981 to 1986, virtually vanished in 1987. Table 7-1 shows the massive buildup of official foreign exchange reserves (mainly dollars) throughout 1987 that was similar in magnitude to the U.S. current account deficit of $161 billion.

Even in the first quarter of 1988, when the dollar recovered slightly in the foreign exchanges and U.S. interest rates came down a bit, long-term interest rates in the United States were still much higher than in Germany and Japan, and thus registered (on net balance) the expectation of further dollar depreciation and higher American price inflation.

The "Tight Money" Interpretation

Has the American government learned the right lessons regarding the importance of stabilizing the dollar in the foreign exchanges in order to calm investors' fears and bring down long-term interest rates on dollar assets?

This question brings us to the second interpretation--and one more commonly accepted within the American government--of what caused the increase in U.S. interest rates in 1987 before the crash.

Because the Fed was so anxious to defend an "overvalued" foreign exchange value for the dollar in 1987, so this argument runs, U.S. monetary policy became too tight and caused interest rates to rise unduly. Hence, according to this second view, unilaterally expanding the U.S. money supply and letting the dollar go in the foreign exchanges is the best way to bring American interest rates down and prevent further falls in the stock market.

From the perspective of a domestic monetarist, a person who believes that the velocity of the domestic money is naturally stable, this tight money interpretation is plausible if one looks only at the sharp slowdown in growth rates of the American monetary aggregates from 1986 to 1987 (Figure 7-4). From the first quarter of 1986 to the first quarter of 1987, U.S. M1 grew by 16.8% and U.S. M2 by 9.5%. Then, from the first to the fourth quarters of 1987, these growth rates fell to 3.8% and 3.2%, respectively.

If the demand for dollar assets in general--and for money in particular--had remained unchanged in 1987, this sharp slowdown in money growth would have created a classic tight money situation that forced U.S. interest rates upward. Hence the complaints from the CEA and the U.S. Treasury that the Fed made a mistake in 1987 by being too tight.

But this tight money argument can be rebutted by referring to the turmoil in the foreign exchanges. In 1987, the general flight from dollar assets also reduced the demands for U.S. M1 and M2. And the increase in American nominal interest rates on bonds and term deposits (a Fisher effect from the exchange rate scare) further reduced the demand for U.S. money narrowly defined. Although U.S. money growth rates were indeed low, the normal growth in demand for U.S. money was so diminished that monetary policy overall was not "tight" in 1987.

Figure 7-4a: MONEY STOCK (M1)

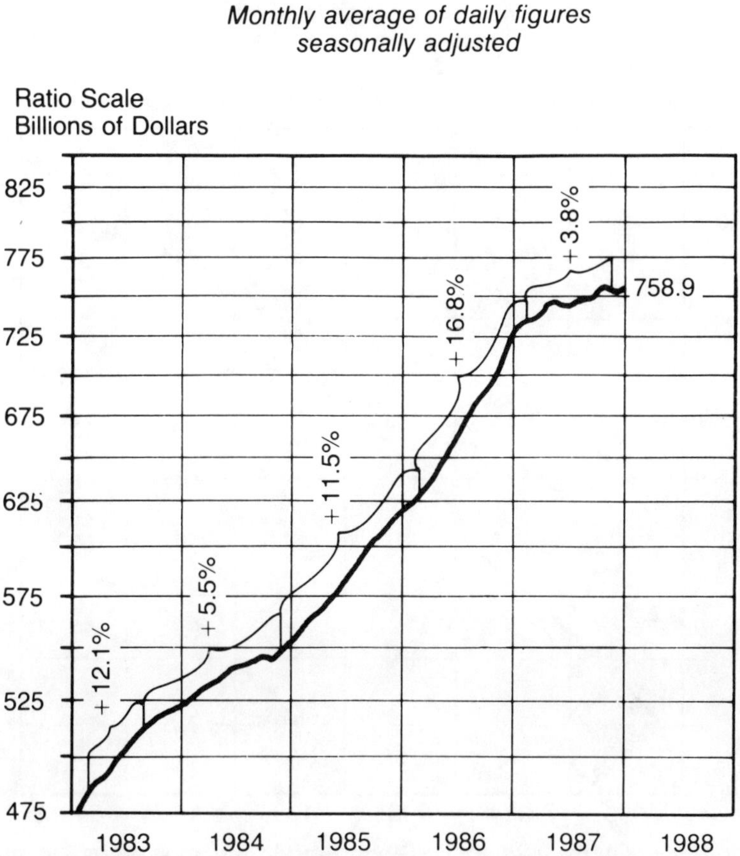

*M1 consists of currency held by the nonbank public, demand deposits, other checkable deposits at all depository institutions and travelers checks.

Source: Federal Reserve Bank of St. Louis.

Note: Percentages are annual rates of change for periods indicated. Latest data plotted: January 1988.

Figure 7-4b: MONEY STOCK (M2)

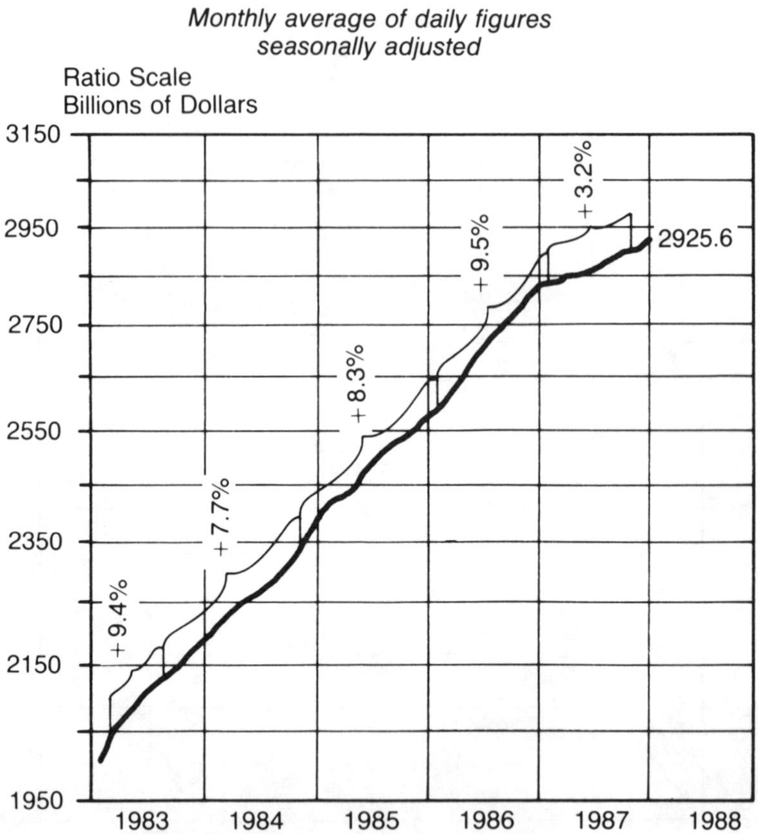

*M2 consists of M1, overnight RPS and Eurodollars, money market mutual fund balances (general purpose and broker-dealer), money market deposit accounts and savings and small time deposits.

Source: Federal Reserve Bank of St. Louis.

Note: Percentages are annual rates of change for periods indicated. Latest data plotted: January 1988.

Indeed, other indicators suggested that the Fed was too easy. When financial markets are highly integrated internationally, and your currency falls against all other "hard" monies, the presumption is that your domestic monetary policy is too loose. Second, the dollar price of primary commodities rose quite sharply in 1987 through to September. Finally, the American term structure of interest rates was quite steeply upward sloping, reflecting the fact that the Fisher effect from expected dollar depreciation was strongest at the long end of the maturity spectrum. In a classic tight money squeeze, by contrast, short-term interest rates increase relative to long-term ones.

As an important supporting corollary to this "tight money" explanation of high U.S. interest rates, a depreciating dollar is seen as desirable in order to increase America's international competitiveness. A domestic monetarist would not want to tighten U.S. monetary policy just to keep the dollar from falling. In this commonly held view, any such depreciation will be self-limiting because it will eventually reduce the U.S. trade deficit.

However, I have shown earlier that, a priori, a currency devaluation has no predictable impact on the monetary (dollar) value of a country's net trade balance.[3,4] Showing why the exchange rate may indeed be an inappropriate instrument for determining the trade balance is a contentious subject that cannot be settled here. Suffice to note that the huge devaluation of the dollar over the past three years has failed dismally to reduce the dollar value of the U.S. trade deficit.[5] More generally, theory and evidence had already existed indicating that the impact of devaluations on the monetary value of net trade balances is ambiguous. Nevertheless, American public officials could hardly be faulted for advocating dollar devaluation in 1986 into 1987 when so many of their economist advisors had adopted an invalid theory: the trade balance approach to the exchange rate.

The upshot is that a trade deficit should be treated as a fiscal rather than a monetary problem. In the American case, the imbalance between saving and investment caused by the huge structural (full employment) fiscal deficit of $150 to $200 billion per year will continue to show up as a large trade deficit of the same order of magnitude--whether the dollar is devalued or not. Although a very serious matter warranting drastic fiscal action to reduce the dissaving of the American government, the dollar value of the U.S. trade deficit is not something that monetary *cum* exchange rate policy can correct--or even significantly alleviate. Nor is it desirable to reduce the trade deficit--the net inflow of foreign saving--as long as the gap between saving and investment in the American economy remains so huge.

Two Perspectives

So we have a direct conflict in economic perspectives. Whether one accepts the "falling dollar" or the "tight money" interpretation of what drove up U.S. interest rates in 1987 determines how U.S. monetary policy should be conducted in 1988. (Curiously, perhaps, these two opposing monetary camps generally agree on the importance of correcting the U.S. fiscal deficit for bringing interest rates down further on a worldwide basis. But the November 1987 fiscal accord between the American administration and the Congress seems too weak and ineffectual to ensure any substantial correction.)

If a lack of confidence in the future foreign exchange value of the dollar is the main reason that U.S. interest rates are so high, a unilateral American monetary expansion in the face of fiscal weakness will fail to bring them down--and cause further declines in the already undervalued dollar that would be highly inflationary. Once the initial effect of the crash-induced shift in investor preferences from stocks to bonds wears off, the U.S. long-term interest rates will again edge upward--with the potential of inducing further declines in the stock market.

This "falling dollar" interpretation suggests an alternative monetary technique for reducing U.S. interest rates (while recognizing the need for the Fed to bail out individual financial institutions in distress). The governments of the United States, the European bloc, and Japan should openly announce their joint intention to put an explicit floor under the dollar in the foreign exchange through monetary cooperation. To prop the dollar up, the Fed should remain relatively tight--but only relatively so. United States short-term interest rates might have to remain high for a while in order to nudge long-term rates down. But once credibility in the new exchange rate regime was established with the resumption of inflows of foreign private capital to finance the American trade deficit, interest rates on dollar assets could be reduced at all terms to maturity.

What then would be the nominal anchor for the collective monetary policy? The triumvirate would control the supply of liquidity to the system as a whole to prevent worldwide deflation or inflation--as measured by the common price level in tradable goods.[3,4]

Lest this proposed solution seems hopelessly impractical, important elements are being considered by the U.S. Federal Reserve System. In his speech to the Cato Institute in Washington on February 25, 1988, Fed Vice Chairman Manuel Johnson suggested that the Fed was now relying more on information from forward-looking auction markets in order to better stabilize the American price level, as broadly defined by the PPI or CPI, which react with quite long lags to current monetary changes.[6] To determine whether American monetary policy was currently too easy or too tight, the Fed would now weigh (1) the steepness of the yield curve, (2) the strength of the dollar in the foreign exchange market, and (3) a dollar price index of a basket of primary commodities. Johnson noted that all three indicated that U.S. monetary policy was quite easy in 1987.

The missing ingredients are, of course, formal monetary cooperation with other central banks and explicit targets for nominal exchange rates to better stabilize capital flows in the foreign exchanges. But this new program is a promising step in making U.S. monetary policy more internationally oriented.

Notes

[1]Council of Economic Advisers, Economic Report of the President for 1988, Washington, DC, Feb. 19, 1988.

[2]---,"Purchasing Power Parity as a Monetary Standard," Economics Department, Stanford University, January 1988 (unpublished).

[3]McKinnon, Ronald I., "An International Standard for Monetary Stabilization," Institute for International Economics, Washington, DC, 1984.

[4]McKinnon R. and K. Ohno, "Getting the Exchange Rate Tight: Insular Versus Open Economies," Economics Department, Stanford University, December 1986 (unpublished).

5---,"Monetary and Exchange Rate Policies for International Financial Stability: A Proposal," *Journal of Economic Perspectives*, Winter 1988.

[6]Johnson, Manuel H., "Current Perspectives on Monetary Policy," paper presented, at Conference on Dollars, Deficits, and Trade, Cato Institute, Washington, DC, Feb. 25, 1988.

CHAPTER 8

FOREIGN FINANCING OF THE FEDERAL BUDGET DEFICIT: MYTHS AND REALITIES

Robert M. Giordano

Mr. Robert Giordano is a partner and codirector of economic research at Goldman Sachs & Co. His responsibilities include publication of strategy for the firm's institutional money market mutual fund and advising the firm's bond trading department. In addition, he has been a return lecturer at the annual Central Banking Seminar sponsored by the Federal Reserve Bank of New York and is a member of the Japan Economic Journal*'s International Board of Economists.*

Overview

Market practitioners often attribute substantial causal importance to factors that are visible in the day-to-day course of business but that play a relatively small role in reality. At the same time, factors not readily visible or easily grasped, but whose effects may be far more important, do not often get the attention warranted. One recent and important example is the foreign financing of the federal budget deficit.

Practitioners have been and remain fascinated by its more tangible--one might say micro--aspects. These aspects--such as direct buying and selling of Treasury debt--are easy to identify and relate to because they are the substance of day-to-day market life. Interest rate movements are often attributed to foreign portfolio activity. Yet, the more abstract--one might say macro--aspects of foreign financing of the federal deficit seem more significant, even for financial market practitioners. They influence the current and future general level of interest rates in many markets, not only the current rates in one particular market. Inflation, economic activity, and political and economic relationships between countries are also importantly affected, and these can have financial market significance lasting well beyond the immediate period of foreign portfolio activity.

There is, of course, no denying that the micro aspects are real. Foreign investors do purchase Treasury securities directly and thereby help fund the federal deficit. Furthermore, they may have stronger portfolio and different maturity preferences for Treasury securities than do U.S. investors. It is difficult, however, to swallow the market mythology that direct foreign purchases of Treasury securities or the role of any one specific foreign investor in financing the federal budget deficit is nearly as important as many practitioners claim.

In Theory...

Focusing on the portfolio activities of a particular investor in a particular market is not crucial for understanding or predicting financial market changes and trends. Rarely is one investor big enough to disproportionately affect the direction of relatively liquid markets. This is true both domestically and internationally. Capital is fungible and financial assets are reasonably close substitutes within markets and across borders where market liquidity, political risk, and tax considerations are not too disparate. As long as capital is allowed to move freely, local interest rates and the foreign exchange rate adjust to channel this capital to the needy country and sector--both directly and indirectly by liberating domestic savings for use in that sector.

Net capital inflows augment the supply of domestic savings and thereby affect the economy's balance of savings relative to investment. This increase in financial resources and the fungibility of savings, in turn, make it easier than otherwise to finance fiscal deficits and private capital needs regardless of the extent of direct absorption of the public debt by foreign investors.

To the degree that financial assets are not good substitutes, the market-specific effects of portfolio allocation decisions can theoretically be important. If foreign investors' portfolio preferences are different from those of domestic investors, and financial assets are not good substitutes, then a substitution of foreign for domestic savings (for example, a drop in the household savings rate and a rise in the current account deficit) can shift relative returns between different types of financial assets or between different maturities of the same asset. Yet, even in this case, the effects will be mostly confined to the particular market rather than be systematic.

Systemic effects mainly result from the exchange rate adjustment that is often an important part of the budget deficit financing process. The less willing private foreign investors are to hold dollar assets, the more downward pressure there can be on the exchange rate. The less willing foreign governments and central banks are to accept this exchange rate adjustment, the more currency intervention will occur. This shift from private to official capital inflows can have an effect within a specific market, such as that for Treasury securities, to the extent that official institutions have the same asset and maturity preferences as private foreign investors, but also more systemically across all markets to the extent that their preferences differ. If private foreign investors prefer investments in longer-dated Treasury issues and central banks prefer investment in short-dated ones, for example, then significant shifts from private to official direct purchases of Treasuries will steepen the yield curve for Treasury securities. Exchange rate pressures also importantly affect inflation, trade flows, intercountry political relations, and corporate financial policy. By focusing on the market specifics of foreign portfolio investment, practitioners can be distracted from these "big picture" influences that will have a greater and longer-term impact on financial markets than that implied by the micro aspects.

The evidence of foreign financing of the U.S. budget deficit conforms reasonably well to this framework and reinforces the theoretical conclusion that the major aspects of this process have a more important impact on financial markets and the economy than the minor influences.

There is no doubt that overall foreign portfolio investment in Treasury debt has picked up. If the data are believable, however, this activity must be of only minor market significance. These flows have accounted for only a small percentage of foreign capital inflows in the last few years, and they represent a minor percentage of federal deficit financing. Moreover, foreign holdings of Treasury debt are miniscule. Direct private foreign financing of the federal budget is even smaller than official purchases, which underscores the critical role played by exchange rate adjustments in financing the budget deficit.

Since 1982, when the U.S. budget deficit first started to balloon, direct foreign investment into U.S. Treasury securities has accounted for 25% of the total net capital inflow, and only 23% in 1987, as shown in Table 8-1. Much of this inflow, however, reflected foreign central banks' investments of dollars received in foreign exchange market intervention, rather than absorption of Treasury debt by private foreign investors. Private foreign investors' direct investment in Treasury obligations was less than 10% of the net capital inflow to the United States during this period, with an outright lack of interest last year.

Table 8-1: CAPITAL INFLOWS AND FOREIGN INVESTMENT IN TREASURY SECURITIES (billions)

	Cumulative 1983-1987	1986	1987
Net capital inflow	$571.7	$141.4	$160.7
US Treasury securities	142.9	42.8	37.2
Net private purchases	54.3	8.3	-6.1
Net official purchases	88.6	34.5	43.3
Other	428.8	98.6	123.5
US Treasury securities as a % of net capital inflow	25.0%	30.3%	23.2%
Net private foreign purchases as a % of net capital inflow	9.5	5.7	-
Net private foreign purchases as a % of total net foreign purchases	38.0	19.4	-

Source: Department of Commerce, Treasury Department.

Federal deficits directly financed by foreign investors have also been small in recent years. As indicated in Table 8-2, only 16% of the cumulative federal deficit has been directly funded by foreign investors since the dollar bottomed in 1980, and 22% since 1984, when foreign investment in U.S. assets began to accelerate. Private foreign investment has been even smaller--5% overall since 1980 and 3% since 1984. Despite all of the current attention, this is also about the same degree of direct deficit financing by private foreign investors as in the late 1970s.

Table 8-2: DIRECT FOREIGN FINANCING OF THE FEDERAL DEFICIT (billions)

	Cumulative		
	1980-1984	1984-1987	1980-1987
Marketable Treasury borrowing	$624.2	$474.6	$1,098.8
Net foreign purchases	70.8	102.2	173.0
Private	39.9	88.2	119.0
Official	30.9	88.2	119.0
Total net foreign purchases as a % of marketable Treasury borrowing	11.3%	21.5%	15.7%
Net private foreign purchases as a % of marketable Treasury borrowing	6.4	3.0	4.9

Furthermore, foreign investors actually own a smaller share of the federal debt today than 10 years ago. They own 15.7% of the nearly $2 trillion in marketable public debt outstanding, compared with 15.6% in 1982 and 18.7% in 1977. Most of this debt, however, represents official holdings of dollar assets that were accumulated with the proceeds of substantial foreign exchange intervention. Private foreign investors owned only about 4.3% of this debt as of late 1987. Although up from 3.1% in 1982 and about 2% 10 years ago, it still pales in comparison to domestic ownership.

Thus, direct financing of the federal deficit by foreign investors remains small by almost any reasonable standard. This same conclusion also seems appropriate when examining the role of specific foreign investors in funding the federal deficit, even the much-heralded role of Japanese investors.

Many market practitioners strongly believe that Japanese investors are the dominant influence in the Treasury securities market, both in terms of absolute yield determination and their effect on the term structure of interest rates. From the practitioners' point of view, it is easy to jump to this conclusion, because Japanese investors are clearly more active participants in all markets worldwide than ever before. They should be; domestically, they have an excess of savings over investment.

The growing financial power of the Japanese is apparent in many areas. Four of the five largest commercial banks in the world are now Japanese; Japanese banks hold roughly 50% of foreign bank assets in the United States; sub-LIBOR (London Interbank Offering Rate) financing costs for U.S. securities dealers were commonplace before October 19; and Japanese dealers now underwrite more than 25% of all Eurobonds compared with only a trivial participation earlier in the decade. Despite these examples of increasing Japanese influence, however, their presumed dominance in the Treasury bond market and role in financing the budget deficit appear to be more myth than reality.

Although the data are somewhat controversial, private Japanese investors own only about 2% of the marketable federal debt and have absorbed only 4.5% of the new Treasury deficit financing on average since 1983, when they were purported to have started playing a more dominant role. Although Japanese investors do seem to prefer intermediate- and longer-dated Treasury issues, even this portfolio concentration represents relatively small shares of all foreign buying of Treasury notes and bonds.

If all Japanese investment activity in Treasury securities was assumed to be concentrated in longer-dated issues, as many practitioners believe, then the extent of their influence should be reflected in the shape of the yield curve and yield spreads to similar securities in other markets. In particular, the Treasury yield curve would be flatter and yield spreads to other markets wider than usual; yet, not surprisingly, such comparisons show no evidence of significant influence.

The ratio of 30-year to 3-month Treasury yields averaged 1.32 from mid-1984 through 1987, for example. This is virtually identical to the average shape of the yield curve in each interest-rate cycle over the last 40 years. In addition, from mid-1984 to mid-1986, the period when Japanese purchases of Treasury issues surged, the yield spread between A-rated (Moody's) long-term corporate bonds and 30-year Treasuries averaged about 170 basis points, only 25 basis points wider than the average yield spread between corporate and Treasury issues from 1977 to mid-1984, when Japanese investment activity in U.S. securities was minimal. A truly dominant force would have likely produced a much flatter yield curve and wider yield differential than that actually observed in these periods.

Figure 8-1: DAILY AVERAGE TRADING VOLUME IN UNITED STATES TREASURY NOTES AND BONDS

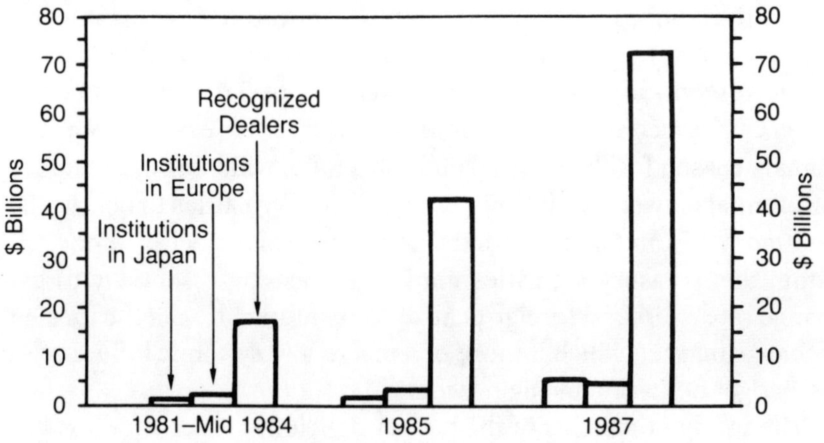

Source: US Treasury Department, Federal Reserve Board.

Furthermore, as indicated in Figure 8-1, the average daily level of foreign transactions in Treasury coupon issues, particularly those of the Japanese, are too small to play the dominant role that many market practitioners have assigned to them. As a share of all dealer transactions, that accounted for by foreigners has fallen.

Either Japanese investors never absorbed the assumed amount of longer-dated Treasury issues in the first place--in which case the market truly exaggerates their influence--or their impact was substantially offset by other factors--in which case the activity of specific investors does not matter much for any length of time longer than the practitioners' daily or weekly operating horizon. To some analysts, and surely to academics, this evidence is not surprising. It is consistent with the long-held view that government bond markets are usually much larger and deeper than the scope of any one participant's cash flows or portfolio activity.

Direct foreign purchases of Treasury debt can still have a noticeable effect on the shape of the yield curve within the Treasury securities market, but such an effect mainly results from exchange rate adjustments. Official institutions generally invest in short- and intermediate-dated Treasuries (five years or less in maturity), whereas private foreign investors prefer longer-dated issues. So, any shift in the composition of capital inflows toward official institutions would tend to steepen the yield curve. An abnormally large $30 billion in foreign official institution purchases of Treasury issues between Christmas Eve 1987 and mid-March 1988, for example, was the primary reason for the unusual and substantial widening interest rate differential between 4- and 30-year maturity Treasuries to nearly 100 basis points from 60 basis points. Although this effect is important within the Treasury securities market, it was due essentially to exchange rate shifts and foreign central bank intervention in the foreign exchange market, which is more of a macro and systemic influence in the budget deficit financing process.

The foreign financing of the budget deficit in a macro context has been far larger and much more important than the direct absorption of Treasury debt that dominates the micro focus of market practitioners. As depicted in Figure 8-2, foreign capital inflows accounted for about 5% of the federal budget deficit and borrowing in 1982, and this percentage has increased ever since. In 1987, U.S. net capital inflows (which are identically equal to the current account deficit) were $160 billion, roughly equal to the budget deficit. The supply-siders were right after all; the budget deficits did turn out to be self-financing! Unfortunately, it was in a way that never occurred to them, a pernicious way that potentially condemns the United States to a prolonged period of subpar economic growth and reduced living standards.

Figure 8-2: THE TRADE AND BUDGET CONUNDRUM

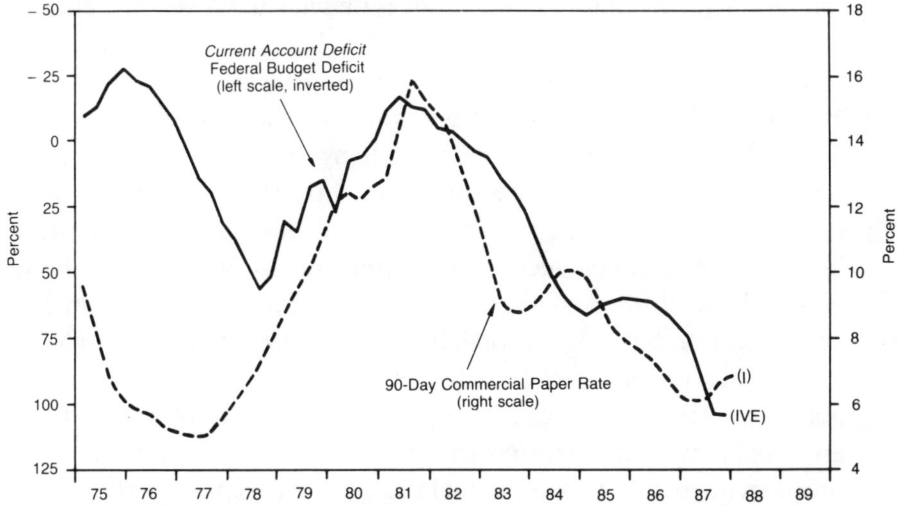

Source: Department of Commerce, Federal Reserve Board.

Note: Data plotted as four quarter moving averages.

This inflow of foreign capital that has augmented domestic savings allowed the large budget deficits to coexist with trendline real economic growth and substantially lower interest rates--a combination that probably would have been impossible if the U.S. economy were closed and such capital inflows did not exist. Borrowing by all nonfinancial sectors relative to GNP has averaged a record 20% in the last few years; yet, interest rates declined on a scale previously reserved only for recessions and sharp falloffs in private and government borrowing. Plummeting oil prices were no doubt a contributing factor. Without such large capital inflows, however, such a benign interest rate outcome would not have been possible in an economy like the United States, with a chronic shortfall of domestic savings and a historically large budget deficit. It would also not have been possible if private foreign investors were reluctant to buy dollar assets and the dollar exchange rate were to decline in the process. Developments in the United States over the past year clearly make this point.

Now that private foreign investors have become less willing buyers of dollar assets, the dominant importance of the macro aspects of foreign financing of the federal budget deficit should become clearer to those practitioners whose attention has been riveted on the micro side of the process in recent years. When private foreign investors are less willing buyers of dollar assets at a time when the U.S. current account deficit is large, the dollar exchange rate falls, reversing the process that earlier in the decade proved favorable for U.S. financial markets. Ultimately, the lower exchange rate also leads to an improving current account balance. By definition, net foreign capital inflows then fall. At this point--the current stage of the process--a smaller percentage of the budget shortfall will be covered by foreign inflows. Unless the budget deficit falls commensurately or business and household savings rates rise significantly, domestic savings have to be attracted away from private sector uses, and interest rates rise. The prospect of unwinding the capital inflow-deficit financing process was probably the essential economic cause of the precipitous decline in stock prices in October 1987. As long as this process continues, the financial markets remain exposed to a replay of the 1987 events, even though any replay would likely be much less dramatic. Alas, there is no free lunch after all.

The lower exchange rate has other effects with longer-lasting financial market significance. Inflation pressures rise and protectionism becomes a seductive antidote to these broader budget-deficit financing effects, as pending trade legislation in the United States suggests. Corporate financial policy is also profoundly affected. A low exchange rate makes U.S. corporate assets cheap in foreign currency terms. This spawns substantial merger activity and causes major corporate restructuring. Although corporate restructuring can increase economic efficiency, it can also cause inequities (cost jobs) that produce political and economic backlash and seriously undermine economic and political relations between nations. Current trade disagreements and difficulties in achieving international economic policy coordination are only two current manifestations of rising tensions.

Being distracted by the micro aspects of foreign financing of the budget deficit in the 1984-1986 period, many market practitioners underestimated the positive financial market effects of the macro influences; likewise, they are probably underestimating the extent of the unfavorable effects. It is not the first time that many of us may turn out to be penny wise and pound foolish and probably not the last.

CHAPTER 9

APPLICATIONS FOR OPTIONS ON CURRENCY FUTURES

Ira G. Kawaller

Dr. Kawaller is vice-president and director of the New York office of the Chicago Mercantile Exchange. After receiving his PhD in economics from Purdue University, Dr. Kawaller served as an economist with the Federal Reserve Board and in industry with AT&T. He also served as a financial strategist with J. Aron Company, Inc. and has been an adjunct assistant professor at the Graduate School of Business, Columbia University. In addition, he serves on the board of directors of the National Options and Futures Society; he is a regular contributor to the Chicago Mercantile Exchange's Market Perspectives; *and he is a contributing editor to "Bank Asset/Liability Management," a professional newsletter. He has also been a coauthor of several books on the subject of futures and options.*

Most professional foreign exchange managers initially investigate options contracts because of the need to manage an existing foreign exchange rate exposure. In this case, the use of options is quite conservative because they are employed to offset the preexisting risk facing the financial manager. At the other extreme, however, options may also be used to take on risk for the express purpose of generating profits. In this latter case, options function as a trading vehicle, and the liquidity of the exchange-traded options markets provides the kind of flexibility and easy access that is quite attractive to those with this orientation.

This chapter provides a concise, largely conceptual overview of these two different orientations to the marketplace. First, it describes the most fundamental way in which hedgers use options; second, it explains how volatility is connected to options pricing; and finally, it discusses the issue of options trading, which, as one might guess, is intimately tied to issues pertaining to volatility.

Options Hedging Strategies

Options limit potential risks to which one is exposed, but they do so for a cost. The purchase of a call option on a currency futures contract provides an offset for the effect of a strengthening non-U.S. currency (i.e., a weakening dollar). Although this strategy allows the manager to limit risk, the market must move beyond a certain threshold if the option is held to its expiration in order for the option to pay off. Alternatively, a put option on a currency futures provides an offset for a weakening non-U.S. currency (i.e., a strengthening dollar). Conceptually, there is the analogous arrangement: One can limit one's risk with this vehicle, and a payoff is generated when the market goes down below some threshold.

Consider the situation of an unhedged foreign exchange rate manager who is exposed to the risk of a weakening dollar. In Figure 9-1, the price of foreign exchange in American terms is shown on the

Figure 9-1: EXPOSURE TO THE RISK OF A WEAKENING DOLLAR

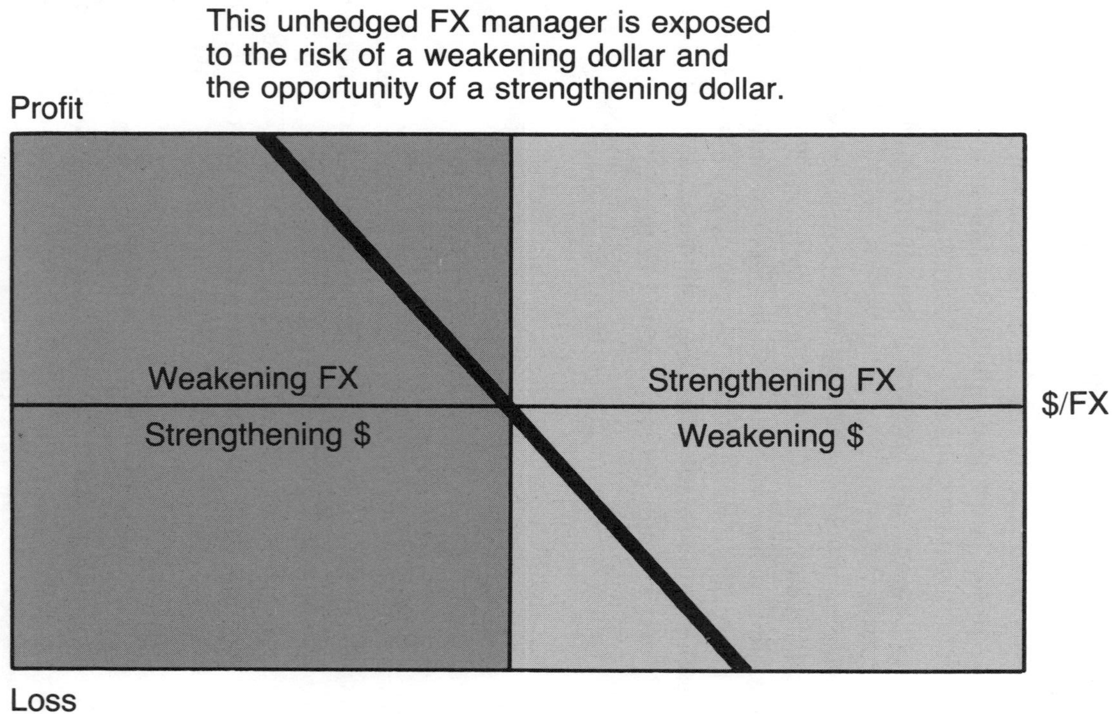

horizontal axis. Moving to the right shows strengthening foreign exchange or a weakening dollar. Moving to the left shows the reverse. If the foreign exchange manager bears this exposure, whether because of the transaction or because of translations consideration, the exchange rate move is either going to make money or cost money. Essentially, this position is nothing more than a speculation that the dollar will strengthen. So what can you do?

You could cover that exposure using futures contracts. By hedging with futures, you neutralize both the risk and the opportunity. An alternative for covering this type of exposure is to use a long call instead of using a long futures contract. If the dollar were to weaken, the option would pay you back for the loss that you would make on your normal exposure. On the other hand, if the market were to move the other way, you would be out the cost of the option, but you might still benefit from the exchange rate move. In other words, by covering with a long call, you can limit the risk and still maintain opportunity. Thus, the effect of buying a call on a currency futures contract is to create a ceiling rate on a forthcoming exchange transaction, with the ceiling rate determined by the exercise price of the option (the exchange rate at which the underlying futures can be purchased) adjusted for the cost of the option itself.[1] When dealing with the opposite exposure, you could manage the exchange rate risk by using the short futures contract or else a long put to get similar choices. In this case, the purchase of a put results in the creation of a floor on the forthcoming exchange rate, or a minimum exchange rate, expressed in American terms.

Issues of Volatility

Although most managers who deal with options recognize that option prices can be divided between time and intrinsic value, many ignore the fact that time value reflects more than just the length of time remaining until expiration. That is, it also reflects volatility considerations. It should be clear that the greater the volatility of any market, the greater are the chances that an option trader can liquidate a trade at a profit. For that reason, greater volatility translates into a higher option price, all else being equal. In the short run, this determinant may exert such an important effect on option prices that it can outweigh the effect of a market move.

Volatility is measured and expressed as an annualized percentage. A measure of volatility of, say, 10% implies a 67% probability that the price will change by no more than 10% by the end of the year, a 95% probability that the price change will be within 20% (2 x 10%), and a 99.7% probability that the change will be within 30% (3 x 10%).

To be precise, one should distinguish between *historical* volatility and *implied* volatility. Past data are used to calculate a measure of historical volatility, or how variable the price history of the underlying market had been over some earlier period (e.g., the past 40 days, 60 days, or whatever). Typically, this measure is simply the standard deviation of the daily returns exhibited by the price series multiplied by the square root of 250, which effectively annualizes the figure.[2] Implied volatility is the variable that is derived from the observed option price. That is, given a formula for the determination of the option price (such as the Black-Scholes formula), one could work backward, plugging in all remaining variables to solve for the volatility that would be required to generate an option model prediction equal to the current market price of the option.

Importantly, nothing directly ties implied volatility to historical volatility. In other words, at any time, these two values could be significantly different from each other. Moreover, it is conceivable that historical volatility might be on a declining path while implied volatility is rising. No mechanism in the marketplace necessarily forces the two to come together. Thus, although many market participants have a natural interest in the historical volatility, the implied volatility is in fact the market determinant that has the greatest impact on an options price. For that reason, a projection of implied volatility carries great importance for the option trader.

Failure to consider implied volatility could have dire consequences for the short-term option trader. For example, suppose a trader bought a call in the expectation of a rising market. Conceivably, the market could rise, but simultaneously volatility could fall such that the rise in intrinsic value would be offset by the greater decline in time value. In such a case, the trader would be right on the direction of the market but wrong on volatility, and a loss would result.

Trading Technique

Given the importance of volatility, it is reasonable to consider trading based on expected changes in implied volatility, independent of changes in market levels of the underlying futures. That is, if you expect a rise in volatility, you would buy options (either puts or calls). Conversely, if you think volatility is likely to fall, you would sell options. In either case, if you are a pure volatility trader, you would take the second step of insulating the position from the effects of price level adjustments of the underlying futures contract.

The principal way traders take advantage of an expected change in volatility involves a process called *delta hedging*. The delta is the movement expected in the price of the option relative to the price of the underlying instrument. Delta values fall within a range of zero to one. For example, prices of at-the-money options[3] generally change about half as much as the price of their underlying currencies (or futures), making the delta about 50% for an at-the-money option. In-the-money options have higher deltas, and out-of-the-money options have lower deltas. The deeper in the money the option is, the closer the delta is to unity (in absolute value), whereas the more out of the money an option is, the closer the delta is to zero. At any time, the appropriate size of the spot position should equal the delta multiplied by the face value of the option exposure. Thus, whether you are a buyer of options or a seller of options, you can offset the market impact of a change in the underlying futures price by *delta hedging*.

Consider what can happen if you predict a decline for implied volatility and the following market conditions exist for deutsche mark futures and options:

Futures	*Prices*
Current price	$ 0.4736
46-call	1.68
47-call	1.01
48-call	0.55

If you choose to sell the 47-call as a volatility trade, you need to buy futures in a proportion dictated by the delta of the 47-call option. Ideally, you would use an option pricing model to generate the delta of any given option instrument, but a reasonably robust approximation can be made quite simply. Take the difference between the prices of the options one strike price above and one strike price below the option to be hedged (in this case, $0.55 for the 48-call and $1.68 for the 46-call, respectively, for a difference of $1.13). Divide this difference by the two-strike interval ($2.00). In this example, the estimate for the delta of the 47-call is (1.13/2), or 0.56. (Because the figure is only an estimate, it is recommended that the division not be carried out too far.) Thus, as a starting point, for each 100 call options sold, you should buy 56 futures.

As the underlying exchange rate rises (again in American terms), however, the call option will be moving deeper in the money, and thus the delta of the call option will be rising as well. (Puts will be moving out of the money, and their deltas will be declining.) As a consequence, the price change in the value of the futures position will not match the change in the value of the option position. To hedge appropriately, therefore, you need to adjust the hedge position as the underlying exchange rate varies.

Table 9-1 shows the deltas for a $1.2250 strike call option with one month until expiration and with one week until expiration, over a range of prices for the spot exchange rate. In addition to demonstrating the rather significant sensitivity of the *delta* to changing market conditions, the table also shows a similar sensitivity to time. That is, even if the market does not change, the mere passage of time will foster the need for readjusting. For in-the-money options, deltas will rise with the passage of time, requiring ever-increasing hedge positions (all else remaining equal), whereas for out-of-the-money options, deltas will fall, requiring a reduction of hedge positions.

Table 9-1: THEORETICAL DELTAS

		CME Option Deltas ($1.2250-Strike)	
Spot Price	Percentage Change in Spot Price	One Month Before Expiration	One Week Before Expiration
1.1070	-10.00	15.48	0.51
1.1378	-7.50	23.21	3.09
1.1685	-5.00	32.44	11.75
1.1993	-2.50	42.61	29.97
1.2300	0.00	53.00	54.77
1.2607	2.50	62.91	77.28
1.2915	5.00	71.79	91.28
1.3223	7.50	79.28	97.40
1.3530	10.00	85.26	99.33

The difficulty in such trading practices is knowing when to adjust. Whether the market goes up or down, failure to adjust the hedge may result in losses--unless the market reverses itself.[4] Moreover, even if a reversal occurs, if such a reversal follows an adjustment, the hedger suffers from whipsaw losses. For example, suppose the market rallies, calling for additional long futures. Then suppose the market drops back. Upon rebalancing the delta hedge a second time, you realize losses on the "extra" futures sold at a lower price. Thus, although volatility trading may offer some attractive profit opportunities, that outcome is by no means certain. The growth of these markets, however, suggests that the opportunities have been ample, and perhaps worth a look.

Conclusion

This discussion is a very basic foundation to help you begin to appreciate the two very different approaches to the currency futures market taken by hedgers on one hand and traders on the other. In this brief space, I have been able only to outline the starting points for the two respective orientations. Still, these comments may have been sufficient to justify further study and investigation on your part.

Notes

[1] The ceiling rate is a maximum exchange rate when expressed in American terms (i.e., dollars per non-U.S. currency unit).

[2] Various models may have a somewhat different multiplier to the standard deviation, depending on the number of observations per year. For example, a model using weekly data would have a multiplier of the square root of 52.

[3] An "at-the-money option" is an option that has a strike price equal to the current market value of the underlying instrument (e.g., a $1.2500 strike option on the British pound futures is at the money when pound futures are trading at $1.2500 per unit). When pound futures are trading higher, the $1.2500 strike call is in the money and the put is out of the money. When pound futures are less, the $1.2500 strike call is out of the money, and the $1.2500 strike put is in the money.

[4] Consider the case of hedging short calls with futures, with a rising market and no hedge ratio adjustment. As the delta of the calls increases, losses on the calls will exceed gains on futures. In a declining market, as the delta of the calls decreases, gains on the calls will fall short of the losses on the futures. In contrast, delta hedging long option positions permits profits to accrue when markets move either way but no hedge ratio adjustment is made. This latter opportunity comes at a cost, however, maintaining long options will "cost" the holder the eroding time value.

PART III

BANKING AND SECURITIES MARKETS

CHAPTER 10

FINANCIAL MARKETS AND FOREIGN INVESTMENT IN THE UNITED STATES

Stephen C. Eyre

Dr. Eyre is executive director of the John A. Hartford Foundation. His career has focused on corporate and international lending in the United States, Europe, Canada, and the Caribbean, beginning with his long and distinguished association with Citibank. Dr. Eyre's active association with Pace began in the early 1970s, when he assisted in the development of the international banking program. He has been a trustee of the university since 1975, vice chairman of the board since 1980, has chaired the Long Range and Strategic Planning Committee and the Management Review Committee, and has served as a member of the board's Educational Policies, Budget, and Executive Committees. Dr. Eyre earned degrees from Yale University and the Graduate School of Banking at the University of Wisconsin.

We have heard a lot about the financial markets and the test that they have been put to. In the first few weeks after October 19, 1987, we all breathed a sigh of relief that we had a financial market. Since then there has been much discussion about the financial markets and ways to make them better. Despite all the pressures, the markets *did* continue to operate. In retrospect, however, we saw how close they came to closing, particularly the New York Stock Exchange. The *Brady Report* and later discussions have given us a great deal more information on the events that took place in the days both before and after October 19, 1987. I work in a foundation, and we manage several hundred million dollars of assets that produce the income that enables our foundation to make grants. During the summer of 1987, when we were talking to our investment managers, they said that they thought if there was going to be trouble in the financial markets, it would come from Japan and certainly not from the United States or from Europe. How wrong they were! As Jeffrey Garten states in Chapter 13, the Japanese asked after October 19, "What crash?" We wonder what happened in our markets, and we have all read the reports and read the papers. People did not answer phones, they blamed it on program trading, the specialists were protecting their wallets, and you can go on and on. Anybody you talk to who lives and works around Wall Street or the other financial areas of the world has his or her own remarks to make about the whole plethora of things that went wrong over that period. But the system did not collapse totally, albeit the Hong Kong market did close for a number of days. I wonder if the people who run that market wish they had not done that.

John Winthrop Wright poses a good question in Chapter 3: "Have we seen the end?" Wright has gained a lot of wisdom by living longer than some of us and by having seen some of the things that can happen. I think we all have to hope that it will not happen again. We must conduct our affairs so it *will not* happen again. Our markets have to be cared for, they have to be looked after. We must give some thought as to just how much regulation we *should* have (as discussed by Dr. Garten) and *can* have as opposed to total freedom in the marketplace.

Despite the uncertainties in the world today, the United States is a very, very good country in which to have one's assets. The actions of many of the countries around the world attest to that. We're going through a lot of great uncertainty at this time. We're going through uncertainty in Europe with regard to new treaties that will change the way the defense systems of the world work. As we go down the road in the Far East, we're looking at Hong Kong being taken over ultimately by China. We're looking at troubled times in Central America. The world is still far from stable. For all these reasons and a lot more, the United States is, as many people have said, a safe haven for investment. It is also the country that many people aspire to live in. We read in the papers of people leaving Hong Kong and moving to this continent. They wish not only to get their assets out but, in fact, to protect themselves. We have to welcome this investment from abroad; it has done tremendous things over the years for our country, as we all know. We should not, though, be as dependent on it as we seem to be today. We have to get our own house in order as quickly as possible so that we can reap the benefits of this foreign investment while not having to depend on it totally. It puts us in an extremely difficult position to have to depend on the goodwill of foreigners for the maintenance of our financial markets. I hope that one of the things that will come out of all this as we move ahead is a greater realization that if we do not put our own house in order we will continue to live on the edge of the precipice and to manage by crisis rather than by forward-looking activity and planning. We cannot isolate ourselves. We are part of a much greater market, the worldwide market. By strengthening ourselves internally, we can benefit from the breadth of that market without being held hostage to its vagaries.

CHAPTER 11

OUT FROM COMPETENCE: COMMERCIAL AND INVESTMENT BANKS IN THE 1990s

Philip D. Sherman

Mr. Sherman is senior vice-president and a member of the sector staff of Citicorp Investment Bank concerned with strategic questions. He is also head of a task force on Citicorp's internal financial structure. Mr. Sherman has had a long career in international banking and has served as head of Citibank institutional and investment banking operations in Germany, Italy, and Korea. He was area corporate officer in Seoul from 1974 to 1978, a period during which the bank was heavily active in raising international capital for Korean customers as well as expanding its domestic operations. Before leaving Korea for Italy, he was awarded the Republic of Korea's Order of Diplomatic Merit. He is a graduate of the University of Michigan and the Harvard Business School.

Other chapters in this book discuss the coming shape of the world economy and financial system. In this chapter, we look ahead in an institutional sense and discuss commercial banks and investment banks in the 1990s. Although the Glass-Steagall Act has yet to be repealed, it seems to be becoming a nonissue--at least in the way it is most often discussed, which is as it affects underwriting. So-called commercial banks are going to be able to extend their product lines to various underwriting businesses in the 1990s, and so-called investment banks are going to be making more loans. In the United States, as indeed all around the world, the real issue is the competition for management of the saver's dollar, deutsche mark, or yen. This involves a far broader field, notably the split between banking and insurance. So far the leaders in this, the real game, seem to be the mutual fund companies that manage the money for the least cost. That is something all established institutions should think about.

In fact, if there is a serious "Glass-Steagall" type of issue for the 1990s, it is in Japan, where a combination of regulations governing the banking and securities industries, and various rules on interest rates, commissions, and money market activities have so far ensured that *all* the players there remain financially healthy. Consequently, Japanese financial institutions have the muscle to grow worldwide and to adopt long-term strategies in markets where today's margins are low. Competition is almost always beneficial to the customer--in this case, the individual Japanese saver--and we have to hope that this will influence developments in Japan in the 1990s in ways that effectively aid the world's other financial institutions' relative ability to compete.

These are side issues, however. There are certain factors and developments existing today that will affect the financial industry--notice the singular, not the plural--all through the 1990s. We will discuss each of them in turn, stressing that, in looking ahead, we have to think in terms of functionality rather than institutions. Functionality is the customer's viewpoint: The customer cares not about what is inside financial institutions but rather about how they work for him or her. An example is the cash management account. Such an account is a universal *bank*, yet it is really offered by brokerage firms and mutual fund companies. A second example is swap and options markets. In these markets, a corporate borrower or investment client can get almost anything from anybody; AAA companies issue bonds to obtain short-term floating-rate funds, and bank customers can get fixed-rate financing, which previously was unavailable to them if they were not eligible for bond issues.

A second significant general point is that the trends we are witnessing have developed against a backdrop of a major boom in security prices. In drawing conclusions from recent history, we have to be careful not to overstate how well financial intermediaries have performed as a function of their own skills alone. The future outlook is not so sanguine if we assume the absence of quite such a positive environment.

Clearly, the most important financial system development is the *technological revolution*, which has several aspects. First, in the communications revolution, information is increasingly widespread, and it is easy to do business with *anyone* almost anywhere on the globe. Because intermediation depends on some people knowing more or better than others, it is obvious why financial intermediaries are under pressure.

Related to the ease of worldwide communications is the revolution in dispersed data processing. This enables financial institutions and others both to deal with the flood of available data and to conceive and execute transactions that were once impossible. Without these developments, the third aspect of the technological revolution would not be possible either: this is the flood of new techniques involving swaps, financial futures, options, and all the derivative ways of dealing with financial risk and restructuring of cash flows to accommodate both issuers and investors. All these developments are characterized by a decreasing product life cycle.

Technological change made the so-called global market feasible. *Deregulation* is actually allowing it to happen. The trend to deregulation is very strong. It came as a dialectic response to the economic problems of the 1970s. These problems marked the end of the long post-World War II boom, which was characterized by a very stable and regular--indeed, "managed"--institutional and economic evolution. However, deregulation is not necessarily as irrevocable a trend as is the development of technology. Regulation involves laws, and laws can be changed. There will be new pressures on regulation in the financial markets. In the United States, for example, the high cost of adjusting both the savings and loan and the commercial banking industries to new realities will surely suggest to many that it would be easier to hide these costs by some sort of regulation than by passing them through the federal budget in terms of recapitalizations of the FSLIC and FDIC.

The combination of technology and deregulation has led to another well-remarked phenomenon: *globalization*, the 24-hour financial world. It is hard to imagine a retreat to a completely exchange-controlled, uncommunicative world, but equally, the initial response to globalization--which has been the hell-bent construction of "global" financial institutions--may have been exaggerated. The reason is functionality. A customer can get what he wants from the world financial system rather easily these days. Communications are good: If he is important, all the world's financial institutions are calling on *him*. If he wants to sell gilts and buy Japanese government bonds (JGBs), and if he happens to live in San Francisco, he can do this with the best dealer in gilts, the best dealer in JGBs, and the best exchange trader. (He *does* have to work odd hours.) He can even maintain appropriate *relationships* with the suppliers he needs even as he uses several to do one deal. Industrial companies have never felt that they had to buy their steel and tires from the same source, so why should gilts and JGBs have to be bought from the same source?

In thinking about globalism, we do have to remember that most transactions in most markets are between consenting resident counterparties. At the margin, international activity can periodically be very important and we need worldwide knowledge, but in a real sense the "global investor" and "global issuer" are still niche markets.

Globalism, technology, deregulation: All these are elements in the tremendous increase in *competition* that affects all the players and not the commercial banks only. In a technical sense, we see these factors eating into the value traditionally attached to intermediation--a superior knowledge level on the part of the intermediary and a perception that claims on the intermediary, in the absence of such information on the part of investors, were safer than direct commitments to issuers. The weakening of commercial bank intermediaries as a result of the financing problems of the less developed countries exacerbates this general tendency by changing the credit quality pecking order in a substantive sense as well. The phenomenon of competition goes beyond strict intermediation and applies to *all* financial business, whether intermediated or not in the direct sense.

From a systemic viewpoint, the most disturbing part of the development of competition is the conversion of more and more of our business into principal transactions in which there is little margin except for that we can earn from the positions that arise out of dealing with our clients. In a world system that is a lot less stable than it was in the postwar era, it is clear that the successful financial institutions of the 1990s will be the good managers of risk.

As they compete in a global market, meeting new competitors with new methods all the time, the commercial and investment banks are caught up in another broad development that is clearest at this time in the United States, and perhaps in some other English-speaking countries. This is the revolution of *valuation*, which has developed in symbiosis with deregulation. The corporate raider is the symbol of this revolution, but the phenomenon is really much deeper. The old, balanced, relatively static institutional structure of the postwar world has given way to the competitive, value-oriented economy in which survival depends more than ever on the answer to the usual question: "What have you done for me lately?" Companies are being bought and sold, broken up, reorganized--all to improve their performance, to serve their customers better. There is increasing reliance on outside suppliers rather than integrated internal systems. Just as the San Franciscan trading gilts against JGBs wanted to deal with only the best in each business, companies want the most effective services, which are not necessarily provided by their internal departments. Old job rating systems (in our institution, based on people employed and assets on the balance sheet) are giving way to an emphasis on ability to add value...and a real lack of commitment to old ways. This is a rigorous, competitive world, and it would doubtless suit most of us to be able to relax a bit more. But I cannot imagine this will be so.

The reorganization of the corporate structure is giving tremendous business to the financial system, which helps to organize and to refinance that reorganization. And it is gradually starting to hit the financial institutions themselves. Financial institutions realize this...and that, as the deregulation they want progresses, they are likely to be less sheltered from takeover, breakup, and reorganization.

What is indeed the practical consequence for financial institutions of all the phenomena we have been discussing? It is that in the world of the 1990s successful financial institutions will be those that have built *out* from competence...rather than *in* from strategy. Customers' focus on functionality, which can be implemented on a worldwide basis as a result of technology and deregulation and which is encouraged by increasing competition, suggests that no one can survive very well on the basis of offering a widespread, even global service with elements that are not up to the highest standard. Furthermore, the fact that true global market players are still in the "niche" category tends to confirm that mere geographic spread is insufficient. Take the example of the rush into the United Kingdom gilts market. There were lots of people saying that to be an international financial institution, one had to be big in gilts. Well, as it turned out, non-U.K. firms that took big positions in gilts experienced losses. United Kingdom firms that were strong in London still lead the pack. Lloyds Bank, which has no existential need to prove that it is British, withdrew. The others...well, we will see.

If building out from competence makes basic common sense, then the wisdom is only reinforced by the revolution of valuation, which suggests that only institutions and structures that are useful and that genuinely add value to their customers will survive. This is not to suggest that existing players cannot go into new businesses, but if they do, they have to proceed with clear objectives and well-defined performance expectations. At the same time, existing institutions have to shed businesses and locations and clients where they do not add value. Because it is pervasively the case that there are weak competitors in every nook and cranny of the financial market, it follows that the industry as a whole has to slim down significantly. If it does not, then the practice of working for incremental revenue, which leads to price cutting, will hurt everyone.

There are two major implications of this thesis: securitization and cost management.

Securitization in the context of this chapter is really an aspect of the value-oriented unbundling of financial services. Institutions decide--or the market decides for them--that their traditional role of borrowing money to finance assets does not add sufficient value to justify the commitment of equity capital. It is better for investors to finance issuers directly. Intermediaries then become packagers and underwriters. This does not mean they shrink to nothing: Underwriting of large leveraged buyouts (LBOs) credits is an important way, for example, for leading commercial banks to bless credits that can only then be syndicated; their continued participation confirms that the lead manager will deal with problems as they arise. This in turn suggests that bank credit is perhaps a better way to do LBOs than overreliance on the securities markets. Active management by lenders is not a factor in our present credit-rating system, but it makes a big difference to the success of financing over time.

Securitization, in fact, ties very closely to the major institutional development of the times for banks: the new Basel rules on capital adequacy. These rules require differentiated amounts of capital for different risks, on and off balance sheet, in contrast to the existing system where capital should be largely a percentage of the total actual balance sheet. Wall Street already has a complicated set of rules to implement the basic concept of relating capital to risk. Long after the banks have gotten over the initial pains of adjustment, which may mean raising more equity in a market that may be less than receptive, they will have to structure their business in the commercial banking world much more carefully than heretofore. This can only be good. As we go through the valuation revolution, which says that every part of an enterprise has to earn its keep, and as we face increasing competition, which allows little room for slack, the resulting focus on returns is going to be critical, and there is little downside in having our regulatory system reinforcing this. In this context of balance sheet management, securitization will become more rather than less important as we manage our portfolios against a more complicated matrix of rules to ensure that we are always adding adequate value to continue to hold the assets in question. Securitization of "off balance sheet" items is clearly the next generic need.

The key to cost management obviously is to be in those businesses where one adds value, and not the others. Good managerial cost control of those businesses is the second important element. Both cost management activities have a supplemental benefit in that, as an institution becomes more tightly focused, a lot of costs that had previously been devoted to coordination and to managing the interface between effective and ineffective business units fall away.

All of this is pretty tough for many traditional financial institutions, which often have seemed to associate a high level of costs with an image of financial stability to encourage their customers. Well, in the new world, a mutual fund does not have any marble pillars but, rather, well-constructed statements, a good telephone answering drill, and rapid data entry of customer requests. The marble pillars, and probably some of the rental cars and fancy meals, will have to go. More seriously, traditional intermediaries, and not only commercial banks, will have the difficult task of stripping away businesses that they would never get into if they were starting from scratch. In fact, today we can see new players who are in effect doing this from the easier direction by *entering* diversified financial businesses from the ground up, by purchasing competence, and by keeping a minimal level of central coordination. There are lots of risks here, and laws in many jurisdictions will probably limit the trend, particularly to the British area, but it is something to be watched.

The successful competitors of the 1990s will take their motto from the Marine Corps--we're looking for a few good people--and manage them as a coherent, cooperative team across whatever disciplines and borders it makes sense to cross.

Like restaurants and Broadway shows, financial institutions are mainly the product of the people who work in them: the human capital. In the past, balance sheet capital and regulatory position advantages may have obscured this fact. The successful financial institutions of the 1990s, however, those that provide the services their customers want and need, will find and hold the best people for the job. Against all the change we are experiencing, this is a truth that can be both remembered and projected--and never merely imagined.

CHAPTER 12

FOREIGN PORTFOLIO INVESTMENT IN THE UNITED STATES

Jeffrey M. Schaefer
David G. Strongin

Dr. Schaefer is senior vice-president and director of research at the Securities Industry Association. Earlier he was director of international financial policy at the New York Stock Exchange and adjunct professor of economics at Pace University's Graduate School of Business. Dr. Schaefer has published widely on investment, the American economy, and international finance. He has been a member of a Hudson Institute study group, an advisor to the U.S. government, and a consultant to the Tax Study Committee of New Jersey, among many other activities, including seminars, speeches, and congressional testimony on the internationalization of world securities markets.

Dr. Strongin is the Director of International Finance and a research associate at the Securities Industry Association.

The growth in internationalization seen in the 1980s has been spurred on by investors seeking to reduce risk in their portfolios through diversification and to increase performance by seeking higher returns outside their home country. We first briefly review the rationale for investing overseas and then note some factors that have made the United States a recipient of these flows.

Rationale for Foreign Investing

The market crash of October 1987 presents an interesting example of how investors benefit through diversification globally. Table 12-1 indicates that the U.S. investor, if fully vested in U.S. equities, would have seen his portfolio decline nearly 40% from September 30 to November 30. On the other hand, if a portion had been invested in the Japanese equity market, the fall for those equities would have only been 4.6%, lessening the impact of the crash on the investor's entire portfolio.

Further highlighting the value of diversification has been the postcrash performance of world equity markets, with the Japanese market recently exceeding its precrash high. Finally, despite claims that world markets and economies are more correlated than ever, thereby reducing the value of diversification, recent analyses have noted that while there has been some increase in the correlation of the U.S. equity markets with foreign stock markets, it is still low.[1]

Investors can also find higher returns overseas. A U.S. investor who bought U.S. Treasuries would have shown a meager 1.9% gain in 1987 before inflation. Investing in foreign bonds would have been a decidedly better choice. Not only did U.K. and Japanese government bonds post higher returns of 15.5% and 6%, respectively, in local currency terms, but the U.S. investor would have also enjoyed a currency gain, boosting total returns to 46.6% for U.K. gilts and 38.1% for Japanese governments. Clearly, investing outside the investor's home market can often offer superior returns as well as some unique opportunities not available in the local market.

Table 12-1: CHANGE IN PRICE INDEX FROM SEPTEMBER 1987 TO NOVEMBER 1987 (US $ terms)

Hong Kong	-89.8%
Australia	-66.4
US	**-39.8**
Canada	-32.6
Japan	-4.6

Source: *Financial Times-Actuaries World Indices.*

Institutional investors are not the only ones who have sought to diversify outside the U.S. in order to increase returns and diversify risk. For example, there has been substantial growth in U.S. mutual funds that invest overseas. At year-end 1983, there were 29 U.S. mutual funds with global or international emphasis that had assets of $6.3 billion.[2] By the end of 1987, the number of such funds had increased to 83, with assets of $24.4 billion. The growth of such funds is a prime indicator of individual participation in the globalization process. Also, the proliferation of country funds also indicates increased retail investor interest in securities outside the United States.[3]

Naturally, with the interest in nondomestic equities growing, investor activity in foreign equities has increased sharply over the last few years. In 1985, investor activity in nondomestic equities totaled about $400 billion. We estimate that in 1987 gross activity was near $1.2 trillion, of which two-thirds took place in the U.S. and Japanese equity markets. The dominance of these two markets should not surprise anyone when 65-70% of the worldwide capitalization in equity markets is in these two countries alone.

Foreign Investment in the United States: Some Factors

Foreign investors seeking to invest in the United States generally focus on three factors: expectations of exchange rate movements; the stability of U.S. political and economic institutions, both government and private; and the lure of higher returns. More recently, and perhaps as a result of the recent volatility of interest rates and currency rates, the depth and liquidity of the U.S. markets have become an increasingly important factor.

Of course, as the objectives of each foreign investor vary, so will the significance of these factors in determining where the investment will be made. In large part, however, three factors have made the United States a haven for foreign investment throughout the 1980s.

1. The introduction of floating currency rates has made currency selection an indispensable facet of the investor's decision. The importance of exchange rate movements on the international investor's portfolio is demonstrated by examining the path of the dollar from 1982 to 1987. During the period 1982 to 1985, the dollar appreciated 27%. This means that foreign investors who purchased U.S. securities (or, for that matter, any U.S. dollar-denominated asset) would have received a 27% return, excluding the effects of inflation or any price appreciation or yield, by merely holding these assets. The same investor, however, employing the identical strategy from 1985 to 1987, would have seen his portfolio plunge by 50% relative to his local currency. Not surprisingly, it has been noted that, "As currencies today fluctuate generally more than bond prices, the choice of the correct currency becomes even more crucial."[4]

2. The United States offers investors both political and economic stability. That is, the threat of an economic upheaval and/or nationalization of companies is extremely limited, and the political climate is generally not subject to significant change despite changes

in the political party in power. This allows the investor to take a long-term approach when investing in U.S. securities.

3. United States markets also offer foreign investors, at times, a stronger economic climate than their home market and, therefore, a higher prospective return. For example, as Table 12-2 indicates, in six out of the eight years examined, gains in real GNP in the United States exceeded that of West Germany and France.

Table 12-2: REAL GNP (% change)

	West Germany	United States	France
1987	1.7	2.9	2.1
1986	2.5	2.9	2.5
1985	2.0	3.0	1.9
1984	3.0	6.5	1.5
1983	1.5	3.6	0.7
1982	-1.0	-2.5	2.0
1981	0.0	1.9	0.0
1980	1.5	-0.2	1.2

Source: Goldman Sachs International Corporation.

In addition, foreign investors may be attracted to U.S. bonds because of their relatively high yields, as shown in Table 12-3.

Table 12-3: LONG-TERM BONDS

	United States	Japan	West Germany
1987	8.9%	4.6%	6.3%
1986	7.5	5.0	6.0
1985	9.3	6.6	6.5
1984	11.5	7.1	7.0
1983	11.4	6.9	8.2
1982	10.3	7.5	7.9
1981	12.9	7.9	9.7
1980	11.9	9.4	8.9

Source: Goldman Sachs International Corporation.

Examination of Foreign Inflows in the United States

The United States has experienced significant foreign inflows during the 1980s. Beginning with net purchases of $13.2 billion in 1980, foreign investors accumulated a record $86.4 billion in 1986. Foreign investor enthusiasm for U.S. securities, which was bludgeoned by the falling dollar, fell to just under $65 billion in 1987 (see Figure 12-1).

Figure 12-1: NET PURCHASES OF UNITED STATES SECURITIES BY FOREIGN INVESTORS

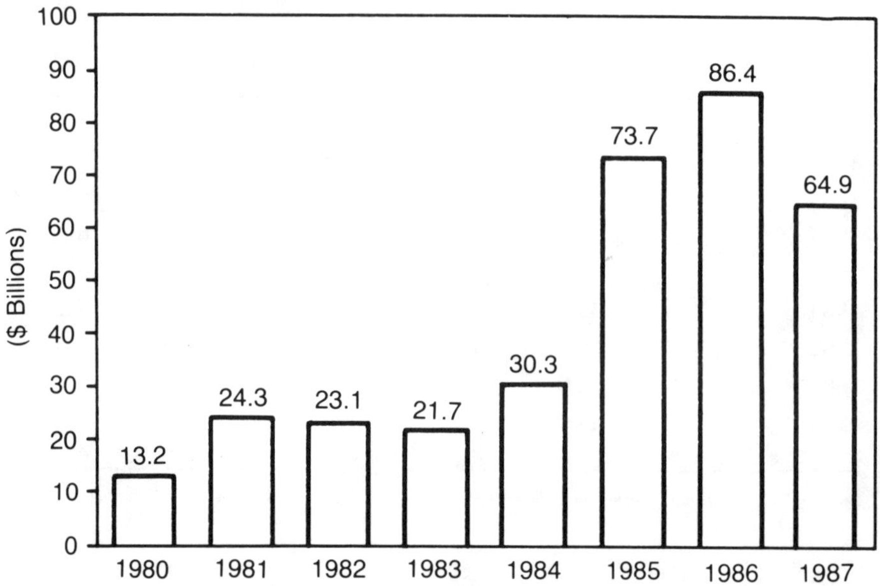

However, a more interesting story is told by examination of the net purchase figures by instrument: corporate bonds, equities, and treasuries (see Table 12-4). Perhaps most interesting of all is that no particular pattern has developed for any significant period. This indicates that foreign investors make relatively quick shifts in the U.S. portions of their portfolios and that trends in the denomination of the security (in this case, the dollar) tend to be an important factor in the investor's decision.

The following offers some explanation for the behavior exhibited in Table 12-4. Suffering from an 18% inflation rate, U.K. investors led the surge in U.S. equity purchases by foreigners in 1980, accounting for nearly half of these purchases. The heavy net purchases of Treasuries in 1981 and 1982 are attributed to the investment of surplus dollars by OPEC countries. Increasing yields on long-term bonds drew investors into Treasuries. There were significant net purchases by "other Asia" countries, in actuality, the oil-exporting countries in the Mideast. Meanwhile, a U.S. recession most likely made credit-conscious investors move away from the corporate sector.

Table 12-4: FOREIGN INVESTORS INDICATE LITTLE PREFERENCE AMONG UNITED STATES SECURITIES

		Percentage of Total		
	Total Net Purchases	Corporate Bonds	Equities	Treasuries
1987	$64.9	35.0%	25.1%	39.9%
1986	86.4	50.3	21.6	28.1
1985	73.7	54.0	6.7	39.3
1984	30.3	39.2	9.8	70.6
1983	21.7	50.2	24.9	24.9
1982	23.1	7.8	17.3	74.9
1981	24.3	14.4	23.9	61.7
1980	13.2	22.0	40.9	37.1

Source: US Treasury.

The removal of the withholding tax on portfolio interest in mid-1984 renewed foreign investor enthusiasm for U.S. fixed income corporate securities. In addition, Eurobonds became a more important financing vehicle for U.S. corporations in the mid-1980s and accounted for a record $38 billion in 1986. These flows continued until about April 1987, when rising interest costs, the declining dollar, and liquidity problems contributed to a decline in corporate issuance. Finally, 1986 and 1987 marked a surge in the healthy foreign appetite for equity purchases. Steadily declining bond yields throughout 1986 and early 1987, combined with a roaring bull market and portfolio diversification, led to significant purchases of U.S. equities in 1986 and 1987.

The increase in net capital flows corresponds with other nations' current account surpluses in the early 1980s. In 1983, their surpluses began to mushroom. At the same time, the U.S. current account posted larger and larger deficits.

Foreign Activity in U.S. Treasuries

The U.S. Treasury market offers investors the world's most liquid and efficient market to trade in. In addition to these market-related factors, the foreign investor's confidence in the political and economic stability of the United States allows U.S. governments to be sold to foreign investors without an additional risk premium. This confidence, however, is fragile and recent publicity about the trade bill and several amendments impeding the flow of foreign capital into the United States would not be lost on foreign investors, who would no doubt demand an increased return or reduce the supply of capital to U.S. users.

Foreign gross activity grew steadily throughout the 1980s and then skyrocketed in 1986 and 1987. Indeed, we estimate that foreign investors account for about 9% of the trading in U.S. Treasuries and hold over 19% of public debt securities held by nonbank investors. Several factors have contributed to this increase, including technological advances, the proliferation of derivative products, interest-rate and currency-rate volatility, the reduction of regulation that hampers capital flows, and the "short-term" approach to making profits that has recently been adopted by many institutional investors. As Figure 12-2 indicates, gross activity in 1987 exceeded 1986 by an impressive 28%. More startling is that 1987's total activity exceeded the combined total for 1980-1985.

Figure 12-2: GROSS ACTIVITY IN UNITED STATES TREASURIES BY FOREIGN INVESTORS AND THEIR SHARE

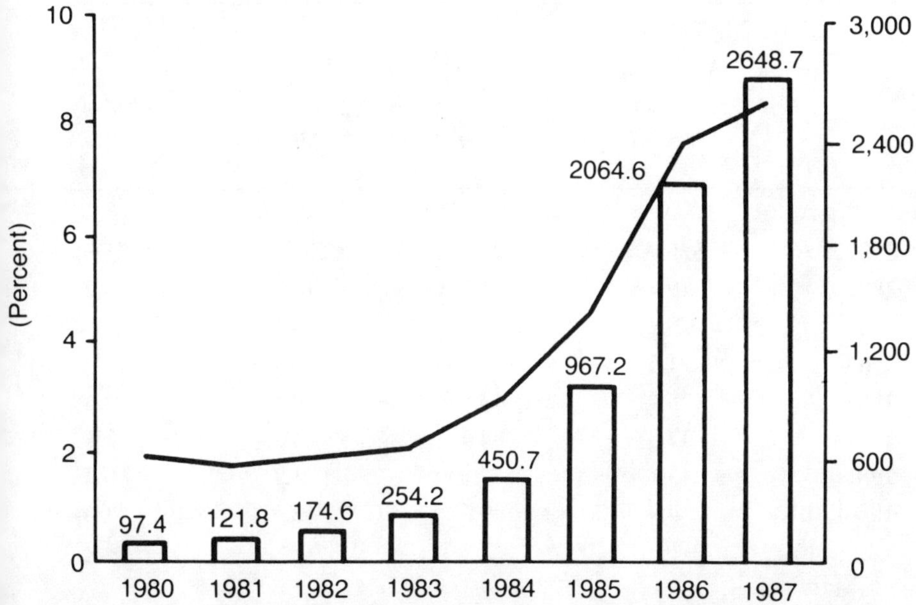

Note: Right axis represents gross activity by foreign investors; left axis indicates foreign investors' share of gross activity by all investors.

Net activity by foreign investors has also grown and helped to finance the U.S. deficit, reducing the crowding-out effect of U.S. deficit finance on the corporate sector. The positive impact of foreign capital on U.S. debt finance can be highlighted as follows: Foreign investors averaged $16 billion annually in net purchases in the 1980s, equivalent to 14% of the increase in U.S. Treasuries outstanding.

Finally, the declining fortunes of the dollar in recent years has had a noticeable impact on the end buyer of Treasuries.

Table 12-5: NET PURCHASES OF UNITED STATES TREASURIES BY FOREIGN INVESTORS--OFFICIAL INSTITUTIONS PROP UP THE DOLLAR

	Total of All Foreign Investors ($Bils.)	Official Foreign Institutions (%)	Official Foreign Institutions ($Bils.)	Private ($Bils.)
1987	$25.9	120.5%	$31.2	$(5.3)
1986	19.4	73.2	14.2	5.2
1985	29.2	27.7	8.1	21.1
1984	21.5	2.4	0.5	21.0
1983	5.4	14.8	0.8	4.6
1982	17.3	84.4	14.6	2.7
1981	15.1	77.5	11.7	3.4
1980	4.9	79.6	3.9	1.0

Source: US Treasury.

Foreign private investors, who purchased over $20 billion in both 1984 and 1985, reduced their net purchases in 1986 to just over $5 billion and actually were net *sellers* of over $5 billion in 1987. Foreign official institutions, in an effort to prop up the dollar, were heavy net purchasers in 1986 and 1987. Indeed, in 1987 these institutions were net purchasers of an amount equal to nearly 22% of the increase in U.S. Treasuries outstanding (see Table 12-5).

Foreign Activity in U.S. Corporate Debt

In the mid-1980s, foreign interest in U.S. corporate debt has also been a significant factor. This was particularly true in 1985-1986 as the U.S. bond market rallied and the foreign withholding tax was abolished in mid-1984. Both gross and net activity peaked in 1986. In 1987, the downward trend in the dollar, as well as higher-yielding bonds offered in U.K. and Australian pounds, reduced the attractiveness of dollar bonds to foreigners as they turned to fixed income securities issued by other nations or in other currencies (see Figure 12-3).

Figure 12-3: GROSS ACTIVITY IN UNITED STATES CORPORATE DEBT BY FOREIGN INVESTORS

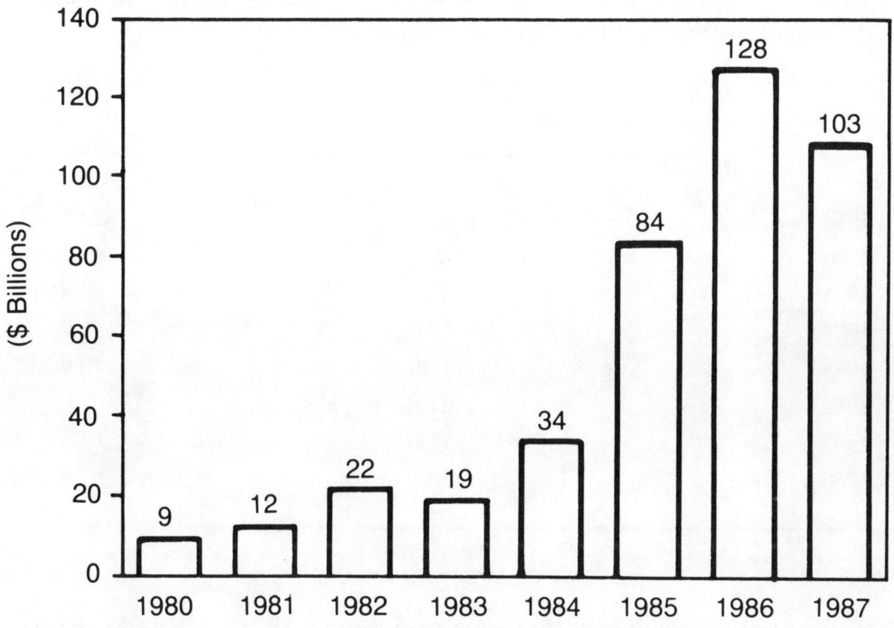

Foreign Activity in U.S. Equities

Similar to that in Treasuries and corporate bonds, gross and net activity in U.S. equities has shown pronounced growth (see Table 12-6). Declining bond yields throughout 1986 and into early 1987 and the diversification of investor portfolios supplied the background for this activity. Gross activity in 1987 reached a record $482 billion, nearly one and three-quarters times 1986's record $277 billion. Similarly, net purchases of U.S. equities increased and reached a record-shattering high of $18.7 billion in 1986. The first three quarters of 1987 promised a new record high, as net purchases stood at $23.5 billion. The October crash, however, led to net sales in the fourth quarter of about $7 billion, reducing the 1987 total to a still respectable $16.3 billion.

Table 12-6: GROSS AND NET ACTIVITY BY FOREIGNERS IN UNITED STATES CORPORATES (billions of dollars)

	Gross	Net
1987	$103.2	$22.7
1986	128.2	43.5
1985	83.5	39.8
1984	34.0	11.9
1983	19.0	10.9
1982	21.8	1.8
1981	11.9	3.5
1980	8.5	2.9

Source: US Treasury.

We noted previously that investors have a shorter time-horizon relative to prior years. This "short-term" approach by foreign investors can be seen by looking at the ratio of gross activity in equities to net activity, as shown in Table 12-7.

Table 12-7: THE INCREASED TRADING ACTIVITY BY FOREIGN INVESTORS IN UNITED STATES EQUITIES (billions of dollars)

	Gross Activity	Net Activity	Ratio of Gross to Net
1987	$482	$16.3	29.6
1986	277	18.7	14.8
1985	157	4.9	32.0
1984	123	(0.3)	-
1983	134	5.4	24.8
1982	80	3.8	21.1
1981	75	5.7	13.2
1980	75	5.4	13.9

Source: US Treasury.

In the early 1980s, gross activity was only about 13 times net activity. This ratio has continued to grow throughout the 1980s and, except for a temporary fall in 1986, easily exceeds the ratio of the early 1980s. Such activity may help explain the increasingly volatile nature of stock prices and is consistent with the dramatic surges in NYSE volume over the last several years.

The increasing influence of foreign investors on U.S. equity markets can be demonstrated as follows: net purchases by foreign investors in the past seven years have totaled an unprecedented $51.8 billion and occurred during a period in which the U.S. equity supply had shrunk by $306 billion. In other words, foreign net purchases have reached record levels at the same time that the supply of U.S. corporate stock has been reduced at a record clip. This coincidence of activity has no doubt amplified the impact of foreign net purchases on U.S. stock prices. Figures 12-4 to 12-6 and Table 12-8 show this activity from 1980 to 1987.

Figure 12-4: GROSS ACTIVITY IN UNITED STATES EQUITIES BY FOREIGN INVESTORS

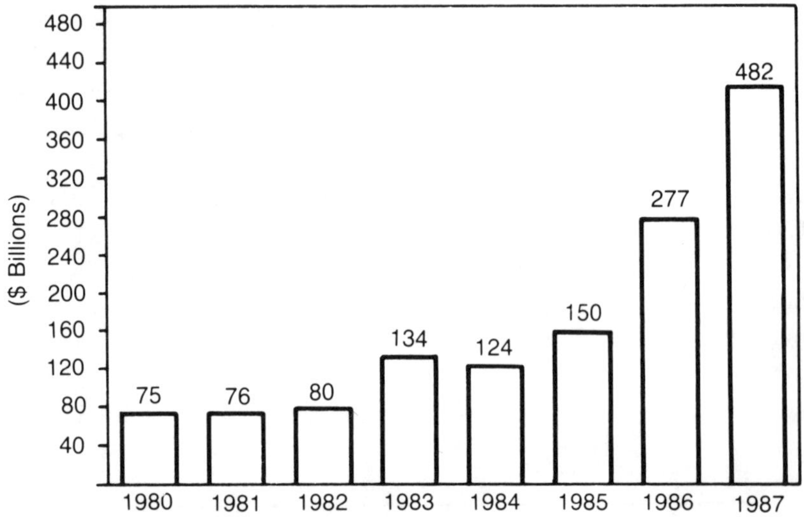

Table 12-8: AS UNITED STATES EQUITY SUPPLY SHRINKS, FOREIGN INVESTORS BUY (billions of dollars)

	Net Purchases of Equities	US Equity Retirements
1987	$16.3	$ -82.4
1986	18.7	-62.6
1985	4.9	-61.4
1984	(3.0)	-81.7
1983	5.4	25.8
1982	3.8	-20.3
1981	5.7	-23.5

Source: US Treasury, Salomon Brothers, Inc.

Figure 12-5: NET PURCHASES OF UNITED STATES EQUITIES BY FOREIGN INVESTORS

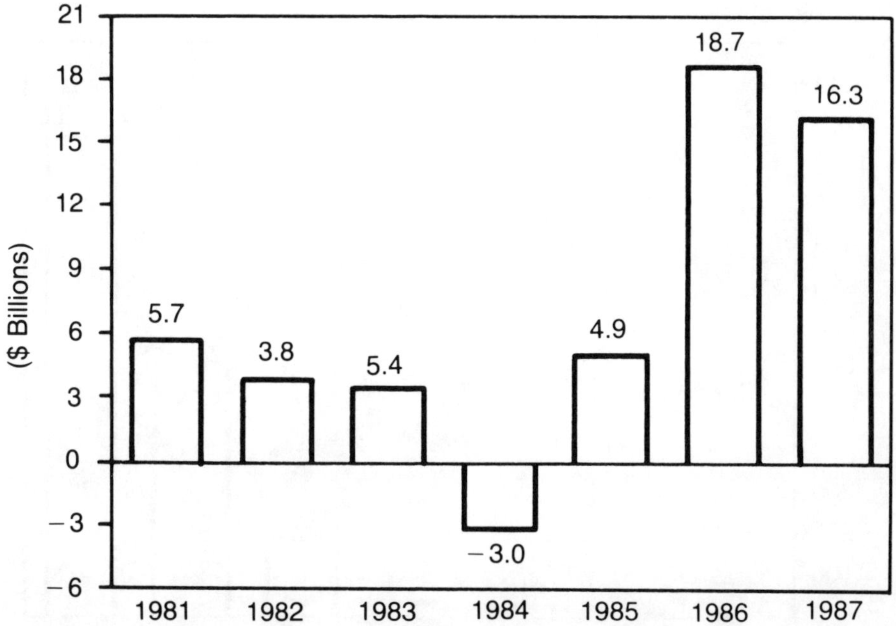

Figure 12-6: GROSS ACTIVITY BY JAPANESE INVESTORS IN UNITED STATES SECURITIES

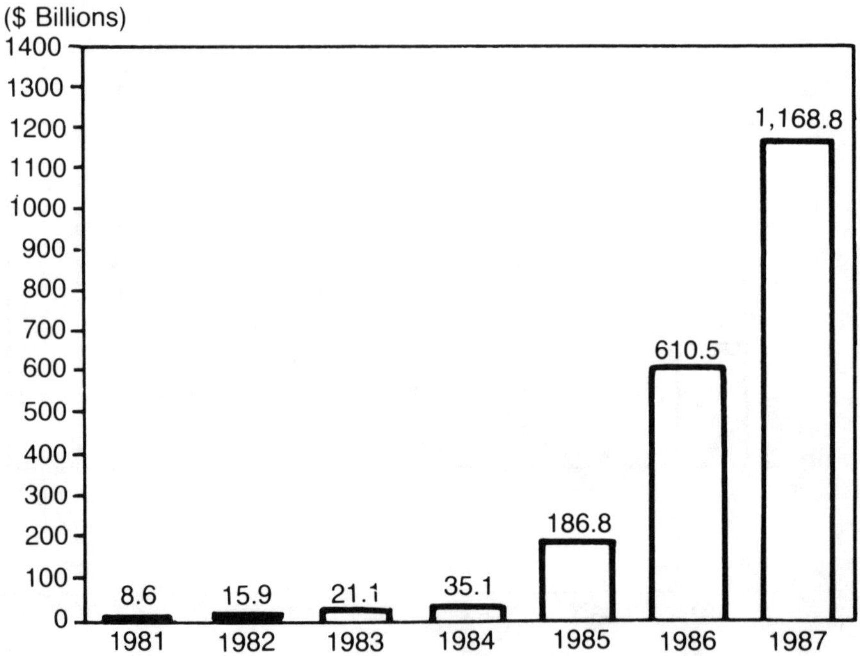

Second, the increasing importance of foreign activity can also be seen by looking at their participation on the NYSE (see Table 12-9). Foreign activity on the NYSE was just over 13% in 1987, a record. United Kingdom and Japanese investors accounted for more than half, after previously never exceeding 30%.

Table 12-9: FOREIGN ACTIVITY AS A PERCENTAGE OF NYSE PUBLICLY TRADED VOLUME

	All Countries	United Kingdom	Japan
1987	13.1	3.3	3.3
1986	12.6	2.7	1.1
1985	9.3	2.2	0.5
1984	9.5	2.1	0.2
1983	10.2	2.2	0.3
1982	9.4	2.2	0.2
1981	11.0	2.0	0.2
1980	11.3	1.9	0.3

Source: Securities Industry Association.

Foreign Holdings of U.S. Securities

Foreign holdings of U.S. securities is another way to show the increased importance of the foreign investor to the U.S. securities markets. During the period 1980 to the first half of 1987, foreign holdings of U.S. securities tripled, from $216 billion to $651 billion. Most of the increase was in corporate bonds and Treasuries. However, as equity prices soared, foreign investors were aggressive in increasing their equity holdings in U.S. securities.

Japanese Inflows

Japanese penetration into the U.S. equity and bond markets is a relatively recent phenomenon. The yen/dollar agreement signed on May 29, 1984, no doubt played a major role in freeing capital from Japan for foreign investment. In terms of gross activity, Japanese portfolio transactions have literally exploded. From 1981 to 1985, gross activity by Japanese investors amounted to $268 billion. This figure exploded by a factor of 2.3 in 1986 and almost doubled again in 1987. Certainly, the Japanese have become major factors in all portfolio instruments, and their trading activity both affects and provides liquidity in these markets. The recent abolition in Japan of special tax-free savings accounts may portend an even further increase in future activity.

Table 12-10: NET ACTIVITY BY JAPANESE INVESTORS (billions of dollars)

	Corporate Bonds	Equities	Treasuries	Total
1987	$ 0.6	$11.3	$ 0.9	$12.8
1986	5.1	3.3	3.8	12.2
1985	3.0	0.3	17.9	21.2
1984[a]	0.7	(0.1)	6.1	6.7
1983	0.5	0.3	2.3	3.1
1982	(0.1)	0.0	0.8	0.7
1981	-[b]	(0.2)	(1.7)	(1.9)

Source: US Treasury.

[a] Yen/dollar agreement signed.

[b] Less than $100 million.

Underscoring the traditionally conservative nature of Japanese investors, Table 12-10 shows that U.S. Treasuries accounted for the lion's share of Japanese portfolio investment from 1982 to 1985. Indeed, on average, 85% of their net purchases of U.S. securities between 1981 and 1985 were U.S. Treasuries. On the other hand, "riskier" equities accounted for only 0.3% of net U.S. securities purchases.

Japanese investors radically restructured their investment strategy in 1986 and 1987. In contrast to the heavy emphasis on net purchases of U.S. Treasuries in the early 1980s, the Japanese investor has more recently made significant net purchases of U.S. equities (see Figure 12-7). United States equities accounted for 58% of all net U.S. securities purchases during the past two years, and net purchases of U.S. Treasuries were cut by more than a third in relative importance to 25%. The declining dollar and diversification have both played a major role in this shift. Finally, we may see additional emphasis placed on equities relative to U.S. Treasuries in the future. The Ministry of Finance (MOF) is currently considering whether or not to relax a law that prohibits life insurance companies from paying to their customers current income out of capital gains. In that only dividends or interest can be paid out of current income, life insurance companies have been averse to purchasing foreign equities, except for high-yielding stocks. If the MOF does relax this law, outflows in foreign equities could be substantial; currently, life insurance companies are the largest Japanese investors in foreign securities.

The portfolios of Japanese investors have been hit particularly hard by the declining dollar in recent years. This had led to a decline in the importance of portfolio outflows relative to direct investment. All trends suggest that unless restrictive legislation is passed, direct investment by the Japanese into American businesses and real estate will continue over the next few years to the benefit of both countries (see Table 12-11).

Figure 12-7: NET ACTIVITY BY JAPANESE INVESTORS IN UNITED STATES SECURITIES

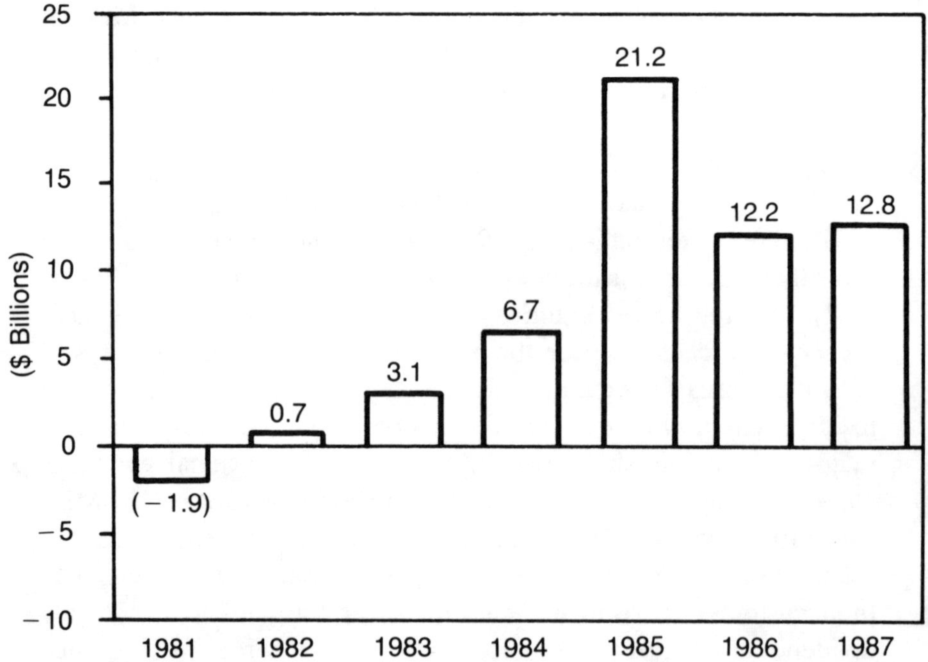

Table 12-11: NET ACCUMULATION OF ASSETS BY JAPANESE INVESTORS (billions of dollars)

	Total	Stocks	Bonds	Direct Investment
IVQ'87	$23.2	$3.3	$7.3	$6.4
IIIQ'87	33.3	3.5	17.1	5.3
IIQ'87	39.6	5.5	25.3	4.7
IQ'87	37.5	4.5	23.2	3.1
1987	$133.4	$16.9	$72.8	$19.5
1986	132.4	7.0	95.1	14.4
1985	81.8	1.0	58.7	6.5
1984	56.8	0.1	30.8	6.0
1983	32.5	0.7	15.4	13.6
1982	27.4	-[a]	9.6	4.5

Source: Bank of Japan.
[a] Less than $100 million.

Foreign Direct Investment in the United States

Foreign direct investment has been on a growth trend following the 1981-1982 recession. After 751 direct investment transactions were identified in 1983, there has been an increase to nearly 1,100 in 1987. Several factors account for this growth:

1. The decline of the dollar, making it less expensive to acquire U.S. businesses or to establish businesses in the United States.

2. Corporations, trying to become more efficient and profitable or to prevent takeovers, have restructured their facilities, making divisions and other segments of the company available for acquisition.

3. Traditional reasons, such as access to large markets and political stability in the United States, have attracted foreigners into direct investment in the United States.

4. Surplus pools of foreign-owned dollars have been and will continue to be available for direct investment in the United States.

5. Foreigners fear protectionist measures in the United States and by investing directly in U.S. plants or buildings feel they can avoid any potential trade barriers that may be set up in the years ahead.

Some indication of the trend in direct investment in the United States by the most important countries is given in Table 12-12.

Table 12-12: DIRECT INVESTMENT PICKS UP STEAM

	Japan		UK		Canada		Total
	#	%	#	%	#	%	#
1986	351	33.4	176	16.7	114	10.8	1051
1985	216	23.7	176	19.3	101	11.1	912
1984	198	21.8	171	18.8	127	14.0	907
1983	105	14.0	159	21.1	97	12.9	751
1982	143	15.7	180	19.7	161	17.6	913
1981	129	10.7	182	15.1	291	24.2	1203

Source: US Department of Commerce.

Concluding Thoughts

Despite the market crash in October 1987 and the flight of many investors back to their home countries while selling foreign equities, recent surveys still indicate that institutional investors believe portfolio diversification is worthwhile. In other words, the globalization of institutional portfolios is under way, and although economic and/or psychological factors may reduce the foreign portion of an investor's portfolio, such factors will not reverse the long-term trend toward diversifying and investing funds in more than one or two countries.

Studies continue to show that correlations between markets reveal that diversity works. Although economies are linked closer and closer, stock markets do not move in perfect parallel; having interests in various markets helps to diversify and provide safety for portfolios. Finally, technology is here to stay, helping to ensure that the trend toward globalization is permanent. We can find out what is going on in other parts of the world almost instantaneously, and advances in communications and technology will continue. Because it is easier to find out what is going on overseas and quicker to communicate, the ability to execute transactions in other countries has become easier, as has access to most foreign markets.

Although some U.S. politicians have raised objections to foreign investment and several writers have played up to fears of foreigners taking over America, we believe amendments to the trade bill will in effect "protect" the United States from protectionism and that the president will be able to sign a bill that continues to increase trade worldwide and keep the United States an open rather than a closed economy. Basically, we believe foreign direct or portfolio investment into this country is desirable and creates jobs. Such capital is desperately needed as long as "our house" is not in order and we continue to run large trade and budget deficits. The alternative to such capital flows would be a lower living standard for all U.S. citizens. Foreign investment in the United States is simply a mirror reflection of the major investment decisions made by U.S. multinationals in Europe and elsewhere in the 1960s and 1970s.

Foreign portfolio and foreign direct investment are simply two aspects of the global village. We continue to believe that such trends are healthy for all participants, both those doing the investing and those receiving the benefits of those investments.

Notes

[1] For instance, "What Is All This About International Diversification and Correlation?", The First Boston Corporation, Nov. 13, 1987.

[2] A global fund is one that usually invests 25% in securities outside the United States, whereas an international mutual fund invests its assets in securities, whose primary trading markets are outside the United States.

[3] We also note that at the time of this publication, two internationally oriented funds, The First Iberian Fund and The Spanish Fund, are expected to list. This indicates that global investing continues apace.

[4] Kidder, Peabody & Co., Inc., *EuroMarkets Prospects.*

CHAPTER 13

REGULATING THE GLOBAL STOCK MARKET

Jeffrey E. Garten

Dr. Garten is president of Eliot Group, Inc., and teaches political economy at New York University. He was formerly with Shearson Lehman Brothers, where as a managing director he was heavily involved in advising foreign governments on their financing and investment strategies. He set up and managed from Tokyo the firm's operations in Asia. Before coming to Wall Street, Dr. Garten held several positions in the Nixon, Ford, and Carter administrations. He is a frequent contributor to U.S. and foreign periodicals. Dr. Garten graduated from Dartmouth College and received his PhD from the Johns Hopkins University.

After trying to digest the extensive postmortems of the October 1987 crash--the Brady Task Force Report, the SEC Report, the General Accounting Office analysis, the London Stock Exchange study as well as stuff coming out of Hong Kong and Australia--I believe that there is one major part of the picture that has yet to be adequately addressed--that is, the *international* regulatory problems and the opportunities for the global equities business. It is this angle that I explore in this chapter.

The various analyses in the United States, the United Kingdom, Hong Kong, Australia, and other countries gave exhaustive explanations of the causes of the crash. In each case, moreover, the international influences were briefly--but *really* briefly--acknowledged. But if you study the reports, what you find is that the recommendations invariably focus only on what happened in the *domestic* markets and only what to do about *that*.

This more narrow emphasis is not surprising. In some cases, such as the Brady Task Force, there was an explicitly limited mandate. In other cases, there were different constraints. London, for example, is hell-bent to become the world's center for global equities trading; most likely no British institution would want to suggest anything about more regulation for fear of scaring off future business. In Hong Kong, there were so many domestic problems that exploring beyond them simply was not feasible. (In Tokyo, where the Nekkei is soaring again, there were no studies. Just a question: "What crash?")

In addition, the international issues are complicated by very different approaches to security regulation in the three major money centers: the United States, the United Kingdom, and Japan. When you add the problems of cultural and legal differences in corporate law, the task of analyzing the global regulatory needs, especially in the postcrash frenzy, would have been too awesome a job even if governments had been motivated to do so.

Nevertheless, everyone knew--and knows--that a global framework for securities regulation is increasingly important. If that wasn't clear before Black Monday, it became clear during the week of October 19 when we were glued to our TV sets and watched the hurricane spread from New York to Tokyo to London and back to our own markets. You can argue about who or what was responsible for the crash, but it is hard to deny that the markets are increasingly linked and that extensive regulatory collaboration among key countries is in order.

It is also hard to argue that enough is now being done to further such collaboration. Yes, there are study groups all over the place for specific issues--accounting standards, settlement questions, and so forth. And our own SEC has commendably been pushing hard to conclude bilateral treaties on questions such as insider trading and seems to be meeting with some success in the United Kingdom and Japan. So often, however, studies and meetings merely lead to more of the same rather than to enforceable action. Moreover, there is no mechanism in place to tie together all the different issues that affect the global stock market.

In short, the effort relative to the magnitude of the potential opportunities in a global stock market, not to mention the potential dangers, is terribly inadequate.

The Need for More International Collaboration

Other than the standard arguments about economic interdependence, there are several specific reasons why a framework for global securities regulation needs urgent attention.

1. More money moves around the world today through securities than it does through the banking system. Although the overwhelming amount of securitized instruments consists of bonds and notes, the equity composition is rising and these flows of money affect exchange rates, investments, prices, and jobs.

2. The equity markets have special characteristics relative to the debt markets. When you purchase a share, you buy ownership and influence on management. Far more than in the case of debt securities,

equity markets are, therefore, subjected to national barriers and a plethora of national laws and customs that constitute great impediments to efficient cross-border business.

3. Unlike bank loans, securities are easily traded at the first hint of change in exchange rates, inflation levels, and so on. Growth in the world's securities markets could well lead to increased volatility in capital flows--with all the negative implications for macroeconomic management.

4. Whereas formal efforts are under way to do something about exchange rate stability, trade liberalization, and capital adequacy for banks, there is no such formalized effort to coordinate securities trading generally or equities in particular.

5. So many of the things that we might like to have happen in our securities markets at home depend on reinforcing actions abroad. To take one example, you cannot have "circuit breakers" here--effective ones, anyway--if markets are open continuously outside the United States. Another example is that it is fruitless to outlaw program trading, if that is what you want to do, if the opportunity exists offshore.

6. Unless certain actions are taken on an international scale, Americans are going to lose out on critical investment opportunities. For example, it is difficult for even world-class companies to issue securities in the U.S. market because of certain SEC registration requirements. Instead, they go to Europe, and U.S. citizens are thus deprived of investment opportunities.

None of the foregoing is news to you, but it sets the stage for our subsequent discussion.

Let us now pose three basic questions:

- What should be the objectives for global securities regulation?

- In terms of an international agenda, what are the most important issues?
- And who should be in charge?

What Is the Global Equity Market?

We should start with the parameters of the global equity market. There is a global market, to be sure, but we should not overestimate its present size or its significance.

There is a lot of loose talk about internationalization and 24-hour trading, but these and other buzzwords evoke an image that is too grandiose relative to the reality. The fact is that the global stock market is still in its infancy.

About 500 world-class companies are listed on several national exchanges, and there are broker-dealers who make markets in shares when the home markets for those shares are closed. Gross sales plus gross purchases across borders may have reached $1 trillion in 1987, but liquidity outside of home markets is not significant. The overwhelming bulk of trades--even in blue chips such as IBM--still occurs on the home market.

The most impressing thing about the global market for shares is its *prospects*. The pace of growth has been brisk these past few years, starting from a small base. It can reasonably be expected that it will mushroom in the next decade beyond what most practitioners imagine. There are several reasons:

- There will be huge Japanese financial surpluses looking for outlets. (Between 1985 and 1987, to take one trend, Japanese portfolio investment overseas increased from $54 billion to $90 billion.)
- We can expect steady growth of pension funds in the OECD countries with aging populations searching the

world over for yield and risk diversification. In the United States, for example, only some 3% to 4% of portfolios are invested abroad now. Trustees with fiduciary responsibility will note that international diversification pays off. Between October 5, 1987, and December 31, 1987, for example, the major stock market indexes, measured in dollars, dropped 27% in New York, 17% in London, but they increased by 0.3% in Tokyo.

- The general trend of market deregulation that is leading to larger and more consolidated markets, most significantly in Europe, will continue. One example of the potential impact is that in London, turnover in foreign equities doubled in the year after the "Big Bang" (deregulation and liberalization of financial markets in October 1986).
- We can expect increasing ease of entry by foreign firms in key markets such as Japan and Australia. Just a few years ago, no foreign firms were permitted on the Tokyo Stock Exchange. At last count there were at least 16.
- There will be many more privatizations of profitable state-owned companies such as British Telephone and Volkswagen, which will add to the world's supply of high-grade, easily tradable shares with international name recognition. Cross-border mergers, within the United States and now in Europe, will also broaden the global equity market.
- There will be greater emphasis in the Third World, especially in the Pacific Rim--on developing viable equity markets to replace reliance on borrowing for growth. The potential here is reflected in the gap between the 30% of world GNP accounted for by LDCs and their 2% market capitalization.

And so the urgency in dealing with the global securities question rests not on the proposition that we are overwhelmed today but that on any reading of the future there will be more and more cross-border investment opportunities. On the other hand, left unattended, the problems will mount.

Objectives

In terms of global regulatory objectives, there is very little difference between the securities arena and conventional banking. In both cases, it is important to increase efficiency by lowering barriers to the free flow of capital. There is also the need, however, to protect the financial system from excesses that damage national economies. Today the safety of commercial banking is far more important than that of securities firms, but, as discussed later, this may not always be the case.

Efficiency and safety, then, constitute the two basic categories of a framework for global securities regulation. The two go together because the more efficiently money can move across borders, the more such movement can cause sudden problems.

The Agenda

In the area of efficiency, regulators should focus on two principal goals, as follows:

1. *Harmonizing standards for accounting, auditing, and financial disclosure.* There is a need to redouble efforts to harmonize accounting procedures among key countries and to agree on minimum standards and common guidelines for making information available on a time-

ly and continuous basis to investors and regulators alike. From an international investor's standpoint, in particular, it is important to be able to evaluate risk and to compare the value of a share in, say, Japan, with one in Germany. There is a long way to go in this area. To cite a few examples, accounting standards vary with regard to the requirement to break down a company's earnings by sector of industry and by geography, the need to consolidate information of all subsidiaries, and the treatment of such items as lease transactions, joint ventures, inventory evaluation, and retirement benefits. There is also great reluctance in parts of Europe and Asia to disclose complete information on issuers--reluctance that has a long history deeply rooted in culture.

To date, the harmonization effort seems to have taken place mostly through voluntary organizations of private accounting firms. To boost this effort, governments and stock exchanges should agree on standards and on more vigorous enforcement. This could be done via statute and through such measures as delisting companies that fail to comply. The point is to put some teeth into standards and disclosure requirements.

2. *Establishing efficient and compatible systems for clearance and settlement.* Inefficient clearance and settlement raises the costs of doing business and decreases market liquidity. The varying problems that stock exchanges have in processing orders constitute a major impediment to the growth of foreign transactions. In some of the world's stock markets, a 40% fail rate of buy-sell orders is not unheard of, and cumbersome physical settlement practices, late deliveries, and physical loss of securities are major risks.

Another type of problem arises out of credit and currency risks associated with different transaction and settlement cycles among countries. These can vary from two to five days in the United States and Canada, for example, to 14 days in the United Kingdom.

Bilateral linkages among markets--such as the links between various U.S. exchanges and Montreal, Toronto, London, and Singapore--help, provided that they result in the upgrading of standards. Regulators could also consider, however, whether to expand the regional security processors--such as Euroclear in Europe, which has done well with bonds--and even whether to go beyond that and set up a more global body.

"Back room" issues do not get priority attention from policy makers. Yet they constitute both the hope and the nemesis of a global market.

It is foolish to pretend that there are not formidable problems to be addressed, even in consolidating national systems, but this is not a reason to do nothing.

When it comes to safety considerations, two other agenda items can be added.

3. *Agreeing on antifraud enforcement.* We need more agreements with other countries to share information and to apprehend those who illegally manipulate share markets. The SEC has made a real start, as mentioned, but it could use a helping hand from other governments that have been yawning on the sidelines.

A model multilateral agreement that would serve as a standard and a goal would not be a bad thing to give some momentum to the job of setting minimum procedures and standards across borders. Of course, it is one thing to have a law on the books, and it is another to enforce it.

Down the road, an international fraud squad with a mission of investigating fraud and disclosing its findings might help to hold national governments' feet to the fire. Then, when Prudential Bache or S.G. Warburg suspected rampant manipulation in, say, Taiwan, it would have two recourses. First, it would ask Taipai to investigate. Second, if the results were not satisfactory, it could ask for a multilateral team to make a finding.

4. *Establishing prudent controls.* Over the past decade, banking regulators have wrestled with one another to establish two kinds of controls over commercial lenders. Following bank failures in Germany and Italy, they have worked to clarify their respective responsibilities as lender of last resort when a bank failure spills across

borders. Next, mostly in reaction to the Latin American debt fiasco, they have agreed to harmonize capital requirements for their respective banks. It is time to apply such thinking to securities firms, through which trillions of dollars are passing each day. One starting point might be arrangements between governments to share information on the biggest global securities firms and their subsidiaries. The big question is: Who should do this? And the answer is: The Bank for International Settlements, which is the established club for central banks in Basle, Switzerland.

Mechanisms for International Collaboration

In fact, coordination of prudent controls raises the question of who ought to be taking the lead in developing a global framework for securities regulation generally.

Start with the United States. Most regulators abroad tend to look to our own SEC as the leader in securities regulation. It would be difficult, however, for the SEC to assume a greater worldwide leadership role even if it wanted to do so. Aside from the fact that it now has its hands full with domestic problems, including the postcrash turf battles among the regulatory agencies, other countries have resented the "imperialist" overtones whenever the SEC has gotten too far out front in proposing international controls.

There are other restraints on the SEC, too, mostly of a cultural and philosophical nature. American security law is not only heavily weighted for protection of the individual investor in disclosures, but it has little to say about the financial soundness of corporations. That is the Fed's job, but the SEC and the Fed are more distant than their respective counterparts are to one another in the United Kingdom or Japan.

The adverse attitude of the Reagan administration toward market regulation has not encouraged the SEC to do much more than react to crises. Anticipating crises, after all, requires some type of planning, which is often seen as being antimarket.

Japan surely has a critical role to play, not only because it has become banker to the world but also because it may now have the largest securities market in terms of capitalization. Moreover, Japan came through the October 1987 crisis so well that it may have more than anyone thought to teach us about regulation, just as it did with respect to industrial management. The reality is, however, that international leadership in any area has never been Tokyo's strong suit.

The European Economic Community is also going to be a major player, much stronger than it was before, as the entire European financial market becomes increasingly unified over the next few years. London is already the major center for global equity business, and the continent has more of an international mentality than does the United States or Japan. In addition, the enormous effort that the European Commission is making to harmonize laws and standards for intra-European financial transactions will give Europe an extraordinary base of experience on which to build. Europe will be too preoccupied, however--perhaps dangerously so--with its own consolidation to give much attention to what countries outside its borders want and need.

Obvious as it seems, there has to be a multilateral effort. Because it makes no sense to create another institution for this effort (it would be a dissipation of effort, at least until a framework is in place), the conclusion is that the Bank for International Settlements should take the lead. It has done so with regard to commercial banking issues. There is therefore some real expertise there.

Some people will argue that banking regulation and securities regulation are not exactly the same and that in any event different institutions (the SEC and the Federal Reserve) represent these markets--at least in the United States. To this objection, there are two answers. First, there is no reason why securities regulators and central bankers cannot sit at the same table. A special committee of the BIS could be designed to do this. Second, and more important, the securities business and banking business will gradually become indistinguishable. Sooner or later, the world stock market will be a direct concern of central bankers.

It is only a matter of time before Glass-Steagall crumbles in the United States. Right on its heels will be its equivalent, Article 65, in Japan. Europe has long allowed banking and securities businesses to operate under one roof. In fact, it is likely that within the next several years some 15 institutions will control most of international banking and securities business on a global scale. They will not specialize in one area or the other--they will each do it all. You will have a hard time telling the difference between Citibank, Merrill Lynch, Normura Securities, and Deutschebank in terms of the services they provide.

Tomorrow's Markets

It is easy enough to make these suggestions. It is far more difficult for regulators to make progress. But the effort must start now, before regulators fall so far behind market developments that they become truly irrelevant.

Difficult as it might be to get action on the four agenda items we have mentioned--accounting and disclosure, settlements and clearance, antifraud enforcement, and prudent controls--these are just the most obvious issues facing regulators. In fact, they are only the basics from which to address the issues on the real cutting edge of tomorrow's equity markets.

The fundamental challenge today is not unique to the global securities business alone but to financial regulation in general. For example:

- How do you keep from fighting the last war, or, more likely, the war before *that*?!
- How do you monitor, let alone react to, the volatile and instantaneous movement of money across borders?

- How do you assess risk in a world of ever-changing financial instruments that the traders, issuers, and underwriters barely understand?
- And how do you bridge very fundamental differences of culture and tradition among countries when it comes to issues such as disclosure and insider trading?

For example, if the eventual dominance of a handful of firms in the world securities markets is a correct view, financial supervision will be synonymous with supervising *them* in the same way that the Fed now watches carefully the big domestic money-center banks. And given the truly global nature of these firms, how will such supervision be done by national regulators? Will there have to be a multinational team devoted to each of these behemoths?

To take another case, it is not science fiction to envision a world market for, say, 2,000 firms that trade in the major money centers with a decent amount of liquidity. This first tier of firms would adhere to a set of common disclosure rules and would agree to certain procedures for international monitoring different from standards and procedures in their respective home markets. Lesser issuers would follow different standards. What problems would such a two-tiered system pose for efficient regulation?

It is easy to envision that many of the stock exchange floors will give way to totally electronic trading, as has happened in London. Institutions will deal with one another computer to computer, placing orders through a "black box" and perhaps circumventing the broker-dealer intermediaries themselves. Then regulators will have a totally different ballgame to referee.

The point is not to dream up new episodes for the Twilight Zone. It is merely that stodgy incrementalism among the regulators will not be enough. But if history is a guide, that is probably all we will get until the next crash. Unfortunately, judging from the yawning that is now taking place on the international scene in reaction to Black Monday, the next crisis may have to be even worse to get everyone off the dime.

SELECTED BIBLIOGRAPHY

Aliber, R. Z., "Financial Innovation and the Boundaries of Banking," *Managerial Dec. Econ.*, March 1987, 8 (1), pp. 67-73.

Allsopp, C., "The Rise and Fall of the Dollar: A Comment," *Econ. Journal,* March 1987, 97 (385), pp. 137-48.

Amelung, T. and Mehltretter, T., "Early Warning Systems in Light of the International Debt Crisis," *Konjunkturpolitik*, 1986, 32 (5), pp. 257-81.

Ariga, K., "On Variability of Exchange Rates," *Econ. Stud. Quart.*, December 1986, 37 (4), pp. 300-18.

Artis, M. J., "The European Monetary System: An Evaluation," *Journal of Policy Modeling,* Spring 1987, 9 (1), pp. 175-98.

Batten, D. S. and Belongia, M. T., "Do the New Exchange Rate Indexes Offer Better Answers to Old Questions?," *Federal Reserve Bank St. Louis Rev.,* May 1987, 69 (5), pp. 5-17.

Belongia, M. T., "Estimating Exchange Rate Efficiency on Exports: A Cautionary Note," *Federal Reserve Bank St. Louis Rev.*, January 1986, 68 (1), pp. 5-16.

Bergsten, C. F., "Gearing Up World Growth," *Challenge*, May/June 1986, 29 (2), pp. 35-40.

Berwin, C., "The European Community: A Union of States without Unity of Government," *Journal Common Market Study,* September 1987, 26 (1), pp. 1-23.

Biasco, S., "Currency Cycles and the International Economy," *Banca Naz Lavoro Quart. Rev.,* March 1987, (160), pp. 31-60.

Bini Smaghi, L., "Dinamica dei tassi di cambio e intervent" ("The Dynamics of Exchange Rates and Interventions"), *Giorn Econ.*, November-December 1985, 44 (11-12), pp. 619-38.

Black, S. W., "Real Exchange Rates and Deviations from Purchasing Power Parity under Floating Exchange Rates: A Comment," *Carnegie-Rochester Conf. Ser. Public Policy,* Autumn 1986, 25, pp. 215-20.

Blackwell, M. P., "From G-5 to G-77: International Forums for Discussion of Economic Issues," *Finance Develop.*, December 1986, 23 (4), pp. 40-1.

Bliss, C., "The Rise and Fall of the Dollar," *Oxford Rev. Econ. Policy,* Spring 1986, 2 (1), pp. 7-24.

Borensztein, E. R. and Dooley, M. P., "Options on Foreign Exchange and Exchange Rate Expectations," *Int. Monet. Fund Staff Pap.*, December 1987, 34 (4), pp. 643-80.

Brainard, L. J., "Managing the International Debt Crisis: The Future of the Baker Plan," *Contemp. Policy Issues,* July 1987, 5 (3), pp. 66-75.

Branson, W. H., "The Limits of Monetary Coordination as Exchange Rate Policy," *Brookings Pap. Econ. Act.,* 1986, (1), pp. 175-94.

Brickley, J. A., "Returns and Risks of U.S. Bank Foreign Currency Activities: Discussion," *Journal Finance,* July 1986, 41 (3), pp. 682-83.

Brunner, K. and Meltzer, A., "Real Business Cycles, Real Exchange Rates and Actual Policies," *Carnegie-Rochester Conf. Ser. Public Policy,* Autumn 1986, 25, pp. 1-10.

Callier, P., "Professional Trading, Exchange Rate Risk and the Growth of International Banking: A Note," *Banca Naz Lavoro Quart. Rev.*, December 1986, (159), pp. 423-28.

Calvet, J., "Le developpement de l'ecu prive figure-t-il un system productif europeen?" ("Is the Development of Private Use of the ECU a Prefiguration of a European Productive System?"), *Econ. Soc.*, May 1986, 20 (5), pp. 101-24.

Calvo, G. A., "Temporary Stabilization: Predetermined Exchange Rates," *Journal Polit. Econ.*, December 1986, 94 (6), pp. 1319-29.

Camdessus, M., "Debt: Are We at the End of the Crisis?," *European Econ. Rev.*, June 1986, 30 (3), pp. 469-75.

Campbell, J. Y. and Clarida, R. H., "The Dollar and Real Interest Rates," *Carnegie-Rochester Conf. Ser. Public Policy,* Autumn 1987, 27, pp. 103-39.

Carli, G., "The Internationalization of Financial and Credit Systems," *Rev. Econ. Cond. Italy,* September-December 1985, (3), pp. 341-51.

Cayton, J. M., "The U.S. Policy Mix, Foreign Financing and the Consequences," *Journal Econ. Issues,* September 1986, 20 (3), pp. 743-58.

Chandavarkar, A. G., "Keynes and the International Monetary System Revisited" ("A Contextual and Conjectural Essay"), *World Devel.*, December 1987, 15 (12), pp. 1395-1405.

Choi, S. R., Tschoegl, A. E. and Yu, C. M., "Banks and the World's Major Financial Centers, 1970-1980," *Weltwirtsch. Arch.*, 1986, 122 (1), pp. 48-64.

Chrystal, K. A. and Dowd, K., "Two Arguments for the Restriction of International Capital Flows," *National Westminster Bank Quart. Rev.,* November 1986, pp. 8-19.

Chu, Y., et al., "Exchange Rates Intervention and Capital Mobility Control: Comparisons and Simultaneous Optimization," *Journal Devel. Econ.,* September 1986, 23 (1), pp. 119-34.

Cohen, B. J., "The European Monetary System: An Outsider's View," *Essays in International Finance*, Princeton, NJ: International Finance Section, Princeton University, June 1981.

Conable, B. B., "The Bank's Mission in a Changing World," *Finance Develop.*, December 1986, 23 (4), pp. 2-5.

Consiglieri, I., "The Perception of Economic Policies and Exchange Rate Dynamics," *Econ. Notes*, 1986, (2), pp. 106-28.

Conway, P., "Baker Plan and International Indebtedness," *World Econ.*, June 1987, 10 (2), pp. 193-204.

Cooper, R. N., "Dealing with the Trade Deficits in a Floating Rate System," *Brookings Pap. Econ. Act.*, 1986, (1), pp. 423-38.

Cordon, W. M., "Fiscal Policies, Current Accounts and Real Exchange Rates: In Search of a Logic of International Policy Coordination," *Weltswirtson,* 1986, 122 (3), pp. 423-38.

Cornell, B. and Shapiro, A. C., "The Reaction of Bank Stock Price to the International Debt Crisis," *Journal of Banking Finance*, March 1986, 10 (1), pp. 55-73.

Corrigan, E. G., "Coping with Globally Integrated Financial Markets," *Federal Reserve Bank New York Quart. Rev*., Winter 1986-87, 11 (4), pp. 1-5.

Crockett, A. and Goldstein, M., *Strengthening the International Monetary System: Exchange Rates, Surveillance, and Objective Indicators,* Washington, DC, International Monetary Fund, 1987.

Cross, S. Y., *Recent Innovations in International Banking,* Bank for International Settlements, 1986.

Culbertson, J. M., "A Realistic International Economics," *Journal of Economic Education,* Spring 1987, 18 (2), pp. 161-75.

Darby, M. R., "International Economic Policy Coordination and Transmission: A Review," *Oxford Econ. Pap.*, November 1986, 38 (3), pp. 545-60.

de Boissieu, C., "L'ECU et la liberalisation financiere en Europe," *Revue Econ. Polit.*, July-August 1987, 97 (4), pp. 435-50.

de Grauwe, P., "International Trade and Economic Growth in the European Monetary System," *Europ. Econ. Rev.*, February/March 1987, 31 (1/2), pp. 389-98.

de Strycker, C., "A Single Currency: Utopia Today? Reality Tomorrow?", *Banca Naz Lavoro Quart. Rev.*, June 1986, (157), pp. 161-77.

Devlin, R., "External Debt and Crisis: The Decline of the Orthodox Strategy," *Capital Review,* December 1985, (27), pp. 35-52.

Dini, L., "Towards a European Integrated Financial Market," *Banca Naz Lavoro Quart. Rev*., December 1986, (159), pp. 377-89.

Dinwiddy, C. L. and Teal, F. J., "Procedures and the Evaluation of Foreign Exchange," *Economica*, February 1986, 53 (209), pp. 97-107.

Dooley, M. P., Frankel, J. and Mathieson, D.J., "International Capital Mobility: What Do Saving-Investment Correlations Tell Us?", *Int. Monet. Fund Staff Pap.*, September 1987, 34 (3), pp. 503-30.

Dornbusch, R., "Exchange Rate Economics: 1986," *Econ. Journal,* March 1987, 77 (1), pp. 93-106.

Dornbusch, R., "Flexible Exchange Rates and Excess Capital Mobility," *Brookings Pap. Econ. Act.*, 1986, (1), pp. 209-26.

Doukas, J. and Rahman, A. H., "Foreign Currency Futures and Monetary Policy Announcements: An Intervention Analysis," *Journal of Futures Markets*, Fall 1986, 6 (3), pp. 343-73.

Engel, C., "The International Monetary System: Forty Years After Bretton Woods: Review Essay," *Journal of Monet. Econ.*, May 1986, 17 (3), pp. 441-48.

Erb, R. D., "Adjustment, Growth and the Fund's Role (Interview)," *Finance Develop.*, March 1986, 23 (1), pp. 15-16.

Feldstein, M., "U.S. Budget Deficits and the European Economies: Resolving the Political Economy Puzzle," *American Econ. Rev.*, May 1986, 76 (2), pp. 342-46.

Feldstein, M. S. and Bacchetta, P., "How Far Has the Dollar Fallen?", *Business Econ.*, October 1987, 22 (4), pp. 35-39.

Ferri, G. and Jafarey, S., "Banking Crises and Welfare Implications of Foreign Lending under Informationally Limited Spatial Horizons," *Econ. Notes*, 1985, (3), pp. 121-33.

Fischer, S., "Symposium on Exchange Rates, Trade, and Capital Flows: Comments," *Brookings Pap. Econ. Act.*, 1986, (1), pp. 227-32.

Fouch, G. G., "Foreign Direct Investment in the United States: Detail for Position a Balance of Payments Flows, 1986," *Surv. Curr. Bus.*, August 1987, 67 (8), pp. 85-103.

Fouet, M. and Aroyo, P., "Petrodollars et marches financiers internationaux" ("Petrodollars and International Financial Markets"), *Econ. Soc.*, July 1986, 20 (7), pp. 15-25.

Frankel, J. A., "The International Monetary System: Should It Be Reformed?", *American Econ. Rev.*, May 1987, 77 (2), pp. 205-10.

Frankel, J. A., "Six Possible Meanings of 'Overvaluation': The 1981-85 Dollar," *Essays in International Finance*, Princeton, NJ: International Finance Section, Princeton University, Dec. 1985.

Frankel, J. A. and Razin, A., "Real Exchange Rates, Interest Rates and Fiscal Policies," *Econ. Stud. Quart.*, June 1986, 37 (2), pp. 99-113.

Fujita, S., "A Critical Note on 'Dollar Standard'," *Kobe Univ. Econ.*, 1985, (31), pp. 69-91.

Fukao, M. and Hanazaki, M., "Internationalization and Financial Markets and the Allocation of Capital," *OECD Econ. Stud.*, Spring 1987, (8), pp. 35-92.

Funabashi, Y., *Managing the Dollar: From the Plaza to the Louvre*, Washington, DC, Institute for International Economics, 1988.

Gebauer, W., "ECUnomics Perspectiven einer europaischen Geldverfassung" ("ECUnomics Perspectives of a European Monetary Order," with English summary), *Kredit Kapital*, 1986, 19 (2), pp. 159-77.

Gerlach, S., "Exchange Rates: A Review Essay," *Journal Monet. Econ.*, January 1987, 19 (1), pp. 137-42.

Giersch, H., "Perspectives on the World Economy," *S. Afr. Journal Econ.*, December 1985, 53 (4), pp. 333-50.

Glassman, D., "The Efficiency of Foreign Exchange Futures Markets in Turbulent and Non-turbulent Periods," *Journal of Futures Markets*, June 1987, 7 (3), pp. 245-67.

Glick, R. and Knaras, H. J., "The Costs and Benefits of Foreign Borrowing: A Survey of Multiperiod Models," *Journal Devel. Stud.*, January 1986, 22 (2), pp. 279-99.

Goodhart, C., "Exchange Rate Economics 1986: A Comment," *Econ. Journal*, March 1987, 97 (385), pp. 19-22.

Grammatikos, T., Saunders, A. and Swavy, I., "Returns and Risks of U.S. Bank Foreign Currency Activities," *Journal of Finance*, July 1986, 41 (3), pp. 671-82.

Griffith-Jones, S., "Ways Forward from the Debt Crisis," *Oxford Rev. Econ. Policy*, Spring 1986, 2 (1), pp. 39-61.

Guttentag, J. and Harring, R., "Disclosure Policy and International Banking," *Journal of Banking Finance*, March 1986, 10 (1), pp. 75-97.

Gylfason, T., "Does Exchange Rate Really Matter?", *Europ. Econ. Rev.*, February/March 1987, 31 (1/2), pp. 375-81.

Hansson, I. and Stuart, C., "The Fisher Hypothesis and International Capital Markets," *Journal Polit. Econ.*, December 1986, 94 (6), pp. 1330-37.

Heller, H. R., "The Debt Crisis and the Future of International Bank Lending," *American Econ. Rev.*, May 1987, 77 (2), pp. 171-75.

Heri, E. W., "Market Efficiency and Forecasting: An Investigation of Foreign Exchange Markets," *Rivista Int. Sci. Econ. Com.*, October-November 1986, 33 (10-11), pp. 1057-76.

Hino, H., "IMF-World Bank Collaboration," *Finance Develop.*, September 1986, 23 (3), pp. 10-14.

Hodrick, R. J. and Srivastava, S., "Foreign Currency Futures," *Journal Int. Econ.*, February 1987, 22 (1/2), pp. 1-24.

Hogan, L. I., "A Comparison of Alternative Exchange Rate Forecasting Models," *Econ. Rec.*, June 1986, 62 (177), pp. 215-23.

Horne, J. P. and Masson, P. R., "International Economic Cooperation and Policy Coordination," *Finance Develop.,* June 1987, 24 (2), pp. 28-31.

Huber, K., "Funding Direct Investment through Cofinancing: The Commercial Banker's View," *Aussenwirtschaft,* April 1986, 41 (1), pp. 89-96.

Islam, S., "The Dollar and the Policy-Performance-Confidence Mix," *Essays in International Finance,* No. 170, Princeton, NJ: Princeton University, July 1988.

Jager, H. and de Jong, E., "The Exchange-Rate Mechanism of the EMS and the ECU as a Reserve Asset: An Impending Incompatibility," *Europ. Econ. Rev.*, July 1987, 31 (5), pp. 1071-91.

Kawaller, I. G., "A Note: Debunking the Myth of the Risk-Free Return," *Journal of Futures Markets*, June 1987, 7 (3), pp. 327-31.

Kenen, P. B., "Exchange Rate Management: What Role for Intervention?", *American Econ. Rev.,* May 1987, 77 (2), pp. 194-99.

Kenen, P. B., "What Role for IMF Surveillance?", *World Devel.,* December 1987, 15 (12), pp. 1445-56.

Kenen, P. B. and Seiler E., eds., "International Monetary Cooperation: Essays in Honor of Henry C. Wallich," *Essays in International Finance,* No. 169, Princeton, NJ: Princeton University, Dec. 1987.

Khatkhate, D., "International Monetary System Which Way?", Editor's Perspective, *World Devel.*, December 1987, 15 (12), pp. vii-xvi.

Korteweg, P., "Exchange-Rate Policy, Monetary Policy, and Real Exchange Rate Variability," *Essays in International Finance,* Princeton, NJ: International Finance Section, Princeton University, Dec. 1980.

Kruger, A. O., *Exchange Rate Determination*, Cambridge, Cambridge University Press, 1983.

Kudlow, L. A., "Loose Money and the Dollar's Crash," *Challenge*, March/April 1987, 30 (1), pp. 52-55.

Lai, C. and Chu, Y., "Exchange Rate Dynamics Under Dual Floating Exchange Rate Regimes," *Southern Econ. Journal,* October 1986, 53 (2), pp. 502-08.

Laskar, D., "International Cooperation and Exchange Rate Stabilization," *Journal Int. Econ.*, August 1986, 21 (1/2), pp. 151-64.

Levin, J. H., "Monetary-Fiscal Policy Assignment under Floating Exchange Rates," *De Economist*, 1986, 134 (4), pp. 467-78.

Lopez-Claros, A., "The European Community: On the Road to Integration," *Finance Develop.*, September 1987, 24 (3), pp. 35-38.

MacEwan, A., "International Debt and Banking: Rising Instability within the General Crisis," *Sci. Soc.*, Summer 1986, 50 (2), pp. 177-209.

Mahajan, A. and Menta, D., "Swaps, Expectations, and Exchange Rates," *Journal of Banking Finance*, March 1986, 10 (1), pp. 7-20.

Marris, S., "Managing the World Economy: Will We Ever Learn?", *Essays in International Finance*, Princeton, NJ: International Finance Section, Princeton University, October 1984.

Marston, R. C., "The Effects of Coordinated Foreign Exchange Intervention in an Exchange-Rate Union," *Econ. Stud. Quart.,* June 1986, 37 (2), pp. 151-64.

Masera, R. S., "An Increasing Role for the ECU: A Character in Search of a Script," *Essays in International Finance,* Princeton, NJ: International Finance Section, Princeton University, June 1987.

McCafferty, S., "Interwar Movements of Dollars to Europe and the U.S. Currency Supply: Comments," *Journal Int. Money Finance,* Supp., March 1986, 5, pp. 5157-59.

McKinnon, R. I., "Exchange-Rate Volatility, International Trade, and Resource Allocation: A Perspective on Recent Research," *Journal of Int. Money Finance,* Supp., March 1986, 5, pp. S113-15.

McKinnon, R. I., *An International Standard for Monetary Stabilization*, Washington, DC, Institute for International Economics, 1984.

Mees, A., "The Monetary Committee of the European Community," *Kredit Kapital*, 1987, 20 (2), pp. 258-67.

Mehran, H., "External Debt Management," *Finance Develop.,* June 1986, 23 (2), pp. 40-41.

Mishkin, F. S., "The Dollar and Real Interest Rates: A Comment," *Carnegie-Rochester Conf. Ser. Public Policy,* Autumn 1987, 27, pp. 141-48.

Miyagiwa, K. F. and Young, L. F., "International Capital Mobility and Commercial Policy in an Economic Region," *Journal Int. Econ.,* May 1986, 20 (314), pp. 329-41.

Mushin, J. D,. "Non-symmetry in the European Monetary System: A Comment," *Brit. Rev. Econ. Issues,* Autumn 1986, 8 (19), pp. 85-87.

Mussa, M., "Nominal Exchange Rate Regimes and the Behavior of Real Exchange Rates: Evidence and Implications," *Carnegie-Rochester Conf. Ser. Public Policy,* Autumn 1986, 25, pp. 117-213.

Obstfeld, M., "Capital Mobility in the World Economy: Theory and Measurement," *Carnegie-Rochester Conf. Ser. Public Policy*, Spring 1986, 24, pp. 55-103.

O'Connell, A., "External Debt and the Reform of the International Monetary System," *Cepal Rev.*, December 1986, (3), pp. 51-66.

O'Donnell, G., "External Debt: Why Don't Our Governments Do the Obvious?", *Cepal Rev.*, December 1985, (27), pp. 27-33.

Ogawa, K., "Some Evidence on the Structure of the Forward Exchange Markets," *Econ. Stud. Quart.*, March 1987, 38 (1), pp. 15-32.

Paulus, J. D., "After the Dollar Crash: The World Turned Upside Down," *Challenge*, January/February 1988, 31 (1), pp. 4-10.

Penati, A., "Budget Deficit, External Official Borrowing and Sterilized Intervention Policy in Foreign Markets," *Journal Int. Money Finance*, March 1986, 5 (1), pp. 99-113.

Persson, T. and Svensson, L. E. O., "International Borrowing and Time-Consistent Fiscal Policy," *Scand. Journal Econ.*, 1986, 88 (1), pp. 273-95.

Portes, R., and Swoboda, A.K., eds., *Threats to International Financial Stability,* New York, Cambridge University Press, 1987.

Pozo, S., "The ECU as International Money," *Journal Int. Money Finance*, June 1987, 6 (2), pp. 195-206.

Prachowny, M. F. J., "Managed Exchange Rates," *Econ. Rec.*, December 1986, 62 (179), pp. 442-50.

Ramanathan, R., "Government Policy with Deficit Financing, Imperfect Capital Mobility and Exchange Rate Effects on the Supply Side," *Econ. Modelling,* April 1986, 3 (2), pp. 147-52.

Rapaz, V. J., "European Monetary System: An Indicator of Foreign Exchange Fixity/Flexibility," *Economia (Portugal),* October 1986, 10 (3), pp. 513-17.

Rofinger, P., "Uber ECUnomics Zu einer europaischen Geldverfassung" ("On ECUnomics for a European Monetary Order," with English summary), *Kredit Kapital,* 1986, 19 (2), pp. 178-83.

----, *The Role of the SDR in the International Monetary System,* Washington, DC, International Monetary Fund, 1987.

Rybczynski, T. M., "The Approaches towards the Reform of the International Monetary System," *National Westminster Bank Quart. Rev.,* February 1987, pp. 2-11.

Sachs, J., "The Uneasy Case for Greater Exchange Rate Coordination," *American Econ. Rev.,* May 1986, 76 (2), pp. 336-41.

Sarcinelli, M., "The EMS and the International Monetary System: Towards Greater Stability," *Banca Naz Lavoro Quart. Rev.,* March 1986, (156), pp. 57-83.

Schwartz, A. J., "Prospects of an International Monetary System Constitution," *Contemp. Policy Issue,* April 1987, 5 (2), pp. 16-30.

Sengupta, A., "The Functioning of the International Monetary System: A Critique of the Perspective of the Industrial Countries" *World Devel.,* September 1986, 14 (9), pp. 1213-31.

Solomon, R., "The IMF in a Period of Turbulence," *Finance Develop.,* March 1986, 23 (1), pp. 41-43.

Stockman, A. C. and Svensson, L. E. O., "Capital Flows Investment, and Exchange Rates," *Journal Monet. Econ.,* March 1987, 19 (2), pp. 171-201.

Stulz, R. M., "Capital Mobility in the World Economy: Theory and Measurement: A Comment," *Carnegie-Rochester Conf. Ser. Public Policy,* Spring 1986, 24, pp. 105-13.

Swanson, P. E., "Capital Market Integration over the Past Decade: The Case of the U.S. Dollar," *Journal Int. Money Finance,* June 1987, 6 (2), pp. 215-25.

Swanson, P. E., "The International Role of the U.S. Dollar under Fixed versus Flexible Exchange Rates," *American Econ.,* Spring 1987, 31 (1), pp. 48-55.

Swoboda, A. K., "Credibility and Viability in International Monetary Arrangements," *Finance Develop.,* September 1986, 23 (3), pp. 15-18.

Tatom, J. A., "Will a Weaker Dollar Mean a Stronger Economy?", *Journal Int. Money Finance,* December 1987, 6 (4), pp. 433-47.

Tavlas, G. S., "Policy Aspects of Alternative Exchange-Rate Regimes: Introduction," *Journal Policy Modeling,* Spring 1987, 9 (1), pp. 1-5.

Triffin, R., "The IMS (International Monetary System...or Scandal?) and the EMS (European Monetary System)," *Banca Naz Lavoro Quart. Rev.,* September 1987, (162), pp. 239-61.

Tyson, L. D., "The Debt Crisis and Adjustment Responses in Eastern Europe: A Comparative Perspective," *Int. Organ.,* Spring 1986, 40 (2), pp. 239-85.

Ungerer, H., Evans, O., Mayer, T., and Young, P., *The European Monetary System: Recent Developments,* Washington, DC, International Monetary Fund, 1986.

Ungerer, H., Evans, O., and Nyberg, P., *The European Monetary System: The Experience, 1979-82,* Washington, DC, International Monetary Fund, 1983.

Van Wijnbergen, S. J. G., "On Fiscal Deficits, the Real Exchange Rate and the World Rate of Interest," *Europ. Econ. Rev.*, October 1986, 30 (5), pp. 1013-23.

Weber, W. E., "Do Sterilized Interventions Affect Exchange Rates?", *Federal Reserve Bank Minneapolis Rev.*, Summer 1986, 10 (3), pp. 14-23.

Wegner, M., "Scope and Limits of International Economic Policy Coordination," *World Econ.*, September 1987, 10 (3), pp. 283-306.

Willett, T. D, "Exchange-Rate Volatility, International Trade, and Resource Allocation: A Perspective on Recent Research," *Journal Int. Money Finance*, Supp., March 1986, 5, pp. 101-12.

Wood, G. E., "European Monetary Integration? A Review Essay," *Journal Monet. Econ.*, November 1986, 18 (3), pp. 329-36.

Zis, G., "Non-symmetry in the European Monetary System: A Reply," *Brit. Rev. Econ. Issues,* Autumn 1986, 8 (19), pp. 89-92.

Zis, G, "Whither ECU?", *Greek Econ. Rev.*, August 1985, 7 (2), pp. 108-24.

INDEX